HV 245 FIE

HOW TO PAY FOR THE FUTURE: BUILDING A STAKEHOLDERS' WELFARE

FRANK FIELD

Institute of Community Studies

In Memory of
Mark Bonham Carter

HOW TO PAY FOR THE FUTURE : BUILDING A STAKEHOLDERS' WELFARE

CONTENTS:

INDEX OF TABLES

ACKNOWLEDGEMENTS

A large number of people helped me in the production of this report. First there have been those who commented either on its first or second draft. Andrew Adonis, Robin Birch, Liam Halligan, Peter Gray, Ed Laxton, and Robin Wendt read through the first draft of the manuscript and Matthew Owen the second. Each provided constructive and detailed criticisms. There has also been a number of people who read about **Making Welfare Work** in the newspapers and wrote detailed letters commenting on the proposals. Some of this correspondence is quoted in the text and I am grateful for the insights these correspondents have provided.

A number of people in the House of Commons Library also helped in providing me with material or calculations. In particular I wish to thank Richard Cracknell, Adrian Crompton, Jane Dyson, Tim Edmonds, Ed MacGregor, Andrew Parker, Jo Roll, Robert Twigger and Graham Vidler.

I wish to pay a special debt of gratitude to Andrew Young of the Government Actuary's Department. He not only undertook the costings in this report but gave me an idea of how public servants can contribute to policy formation. I am similarly grateful to the Esmee Fairbairn Charitable Trust for funding this aspect of the work through a grant paid to the Institute of Community Studies. At the Institute I am grateful to Michael Young,Wyn Tucker and Sue Chisholm for the hospitality they provided for this project as they did for its predecessor **Making Welfare Work**. I would also like to thank Heinz-Albert Hutchmacher and the Friedrich Ebert Foundation for arranging my visit to Germany.

To three people I owe a particular debt. Jill Hendey typed each of the drafts and prepared the final manuscript for publication. Chris Kelsey helped in this task after commenting on the final draft and Damian Leeson challenged the presentation of the argument at every point.

Part of this volume will appear as **Stakeholder Welfare** published by the IEA. The assumptions underlying **Making Welfare Work** are there examined by Pete Alcott, Alan Deacon, David Green and Melanie Philips.

The aim is to publish a third volume considering in detail the technical questions which arise from **How To Pay For The Future** in the early Spring of 1997.

How To Pay For The Future is dedicated to the memory of Mark Bonham Carter. He was one of those rare politicians who enjoyed helping to develop the careers of younger members of the political fraternity. I was fortunate to benefit from his interest, knowledge and friendship.

September 20, 1996

INTRODUCTION AND SUMMARY

One concern obsesses me. The decade before being elected to Parliament I worked for the Child Poverty Action Group. A primary reason for coming to the House of Commons was therefore to seek more effective means of promoting the interests of the poor. But the House of Commons I joined was one where Labour suffered all the symptoms of a party in near-terminal decline. So a concern about the poor was combined with the need to help in the campaign to have a Labour Party which was electable.

The Blair leadership has transformed the Party and its prospects. Until his election as leader I had believed the Party was heading for a fifth consecutive election defeat. But in the attempt to reach those parts of the electorate which were not normally touched by Labour's appeal, a new, equally sombre, dilemma presents itself. Can Labour win the new voters it needs to command a majority in the House of Commons while at the same time maintaining its commitment to protect and promote the interests of the poor? Or will the poor simply be forgotten in Labour's proper immediate concern to build a winning coalition of new voters?

I do believe it possible for Labour both to win and to fulfil its historic commitment to the poor. This was the unifying theme of **Making Welfare Work**, the predecessor to this volume. I do not believe, however, that this dual objective of winning on an inclusive ticket can be achieved without proposing a radical reconstruction of welfare which meets three essential objectives.

First, the significant economic and social changes which have occurred particularly since 1979 must become the weave and the web of welfare's reconstruction. It is not simply that these forces are too powerful to ignore. It is rather that the move to greater freedom and choice which has resulted from many, but not all of these changes is now inexorable and viewed as a fundamental part of the good life itself, not merely as an incremental advantage.

Second, the simple point so long ignored, that human nature underpins all political activities, must become a central determining force in the political debate on welfare's reconstruction. **Making Welfare Work** argued for a decisive rejection of the dominant post-war view, moulded by Richard Titmuss, that altruism was and should be the dominant motive force underpinning welfare.

Altruism has a clear role to play (and, as I will argue, it is still the dominant force in health provision and has here a strategic role) but **Making Welfare Work** viewed it as too frail an impulse to sustain the whole of a modern welfare state.

Self-interest is the great driving force within each of us. No great secular institution can fulfil the objectives for which it was established unless this most basic of observations is recognised and utilised. Self-interest is quite distinct from selfishness. **Making Welfare Work** sought to outline a new welfare settlement which accorded self-interest its proper place in the scheme of things. It also sought to present new institutions through which welfare could be delivered and which accepted as irreversible many of the new powerful social and economic changes shaping Britain as it approaches the millennium.

The third objective centres on the strategy which needs to be employed in delivering a successful reconstruction of welfare. The writing of **Making Welfare Work** and this volume have forced me to think carefully about the process of political change in this country. The idea that all that is required is a repositioning of the 1960s approach to reform is decisively rejected. The model I followed when working for CPAG was to try and harness the sharp-elbow approach of the middle classes so that as they pushed their way to the front of the queue they also benefited the poor. Such a strategy was not absent from **Making Welfare Work,** nor is it forgotten in **How To Pay For The Future**. But a more fundamental approach in building a basis for a successful reconstruction of welfare is employed here which groups welfare reconstruction around that aspect of the status quo with the greatest attraction for the electorate.

Voters attach very different priorities to the disparate policies and institutions which go to make up public policy. And these priorities are clearly different in many of the member countries of the European Union. For many European Member States the role of pensions and other welfare benefits is considerably more politically sensitive than in Great Britain. It is inconceivable, given our political culture, that a British Prime Minister would feel the need to write a personal letter to each pensioner telling them that their state pensions are safe in his hands, as Chancellor Kohl recently felt impelled to do in Germany. Indeed, state pensions in Britain are not safe in the Government's hands. That is why decisive changes are proposed here to the ownership of schemes and their capital. Similarly, it is unlikely that Britain would see industrial unrest erupting on the streets in protest against proposed welfare cuts, to the degree that Germany, France and Italy are now experiencing.

In Britain the touchstone is the National Health Service. This is the one institution which the majority of the electorate regards as politically sacred. Poll after poll shows individuals willing to pay more for their NHS and, perhaps without expressing so directly, affirming thereby their commitment to the one area where altruism is more equally weighted with self-interest. **How To Pay For The Future**'s costings start at this point of great strength. It proposes that the general reform of welfare - moving to a greater degree of insurance-based and individual funding - should be seen as part of a major shift to an insurance tax base in which NHS funding is far more prominent than it is currently.

A basic premise of **How To Pay For The Future** is that people will be prepared to foot the bills necessary for safeguarding and improving the NHS, and other strategic parts of welfare, if they have a control over where their contributions go. There is a belief running throughout this work that the electorate are ahead of politicians in facing up to the fact that increasingly the state's provision of welfare will not meet their needs, and that they will have to resume greater responsibility for their family's welfare. But there will be understandable reluctance to think about meeting higher costs unless the rules of the game are radically redrafted. The schemes must be owned and run by the contributors themselves; they must be protected against the kind of raiding activity the present government has launched against the National Insurance scheme. This is **not** a plea for privatisation. Rather it is a seeking of opportunities to build new individually-owned but collectively-run bodies which are independent of the state.

There is no attempt to underplay the significance of these changes. It represents a decisive break with post-war paternalism. In summary form **How To Pay For The Future:**

- takes the best of this century's social security provision as the basis on which to build the aspirations voters wish to realise in the millennium;

- enhances the position of those in need at the expense of those fraudulently claiming;

- builds a new partnership between the state and the individual in a world where the state's role is being downsized and the individual's wish for greater control over his or her income is increasing;

- transforms a welfare state where means-tests promote idleness, dishonesty and lack of savings into one rewarding work, savings and honesty;

- transfers the implicit individual responsibility to oneself and one's family in general taxation, making it explicit by a switch to an insurance-based contributory system;

- rebuilds a central state operation by new forms of collective provision which are individually owned;

- replaces the growing breakdown of joint endeavours with new organisations fostering social cohesion;

- tackles the growing budgetary crisis by replacing Treasury control over expenditure levels with greater individual contributor control;

- offers greater freedom to the many with protection for the vulnerable.

How To Pay For The Future proposes:

A new social security and health insurance base. The aim is to create a new insurance-based tax system. All earnings over £10 a week will be included and there will be no upper earnings limit (the removal of this bar will be matched by tax reductions). Weekly earnings from £10 up to £60 will be taxed at a reduced rate. The same tax framework will apply to employers and employees. This tax base will initially be used to finance:

- half the NHS expenditure
- a new care pension
- a new insurance against unemployment.

The NHS insurance. Half of current NHS expenditure will be covered by taxing on the new national insurance base. A 7 per cent levy on earnings over

£60 will raise £18bn and this move can be accompanied by about a 8p reduction in the standard rate of tax, or equivalent tax changes.

The universalisation of adequate pensions. In order to achieve a universal coverage of adequate pensions three moves are proposed.

* Under the new national insurance proposals practically every worker will be brought within the scheme and become entitled in their own right to a state retirement pension.

* Workers earning over £100 a week will be required to save towards a second pension.

* The pension contribution of carers claiming the ICA will be made into the state scheme and their own individual fund up to the value of earnings of £150 a week - the sum they will be able to draw as a carer under the second stage of the new care pension proposals.

An adequate pension cover. For workers earning up to £100 a week the state retirement pension, currently £61.15, provides a reasonable replacement retirement income. All workers will be able to continue contributing to their company or private pension schemes. If they earn over £100 a week and are not in an occupational scheme, or already in a personal pension, they will begin to save contributions towards that second pension. **The aim is to give every worker a minimum pension entitlement of two-thirds of previous earnings.**

The closure of SERPS. The new proposals will come into effect at the millennium. At that date SERPS will be closed and there will be no further accruals of SERPS. The initial contribution rate to the second pension will be set at 4.6 per cent, the same extra NI contribution as will effectively be paid by those people in SERPS in 2000. Over time this 4.6 per cent contribution to a personal pension fund will need to be increased to 16 per cent for those workers not yet making this size of contribution, or in an occupational scheme which it is assumed will provide benefits equivalent to this rate of saving. Savers will be free to use private companies or mutually-aided bodies as the vehicle for their savings.

The closure of SERPS will lead to considerable savings in pension expenditure.

The fall in the projected costs of SERPS begins in 2001-2, although the fall will be very modest in that initial year.

- By 2020, however, the fall in expenditure over current projections, based on no change to SERPS, will amount to £2bn. By the year 2050 the lowered expenditure level will be equal to £7bn a year. Current and future taxpayers will not only be increasingly covering the cost of their own future pensions but they will also have to continue to meet SERPS entitlements which have already accrued.

- It is therefore proposed that these future gains be shared with the current generation who otherwise pay twice, ie for their own pension and for past pension commitments to other workers.

- The proposal is for bonds to be issued annually which will finance the future increase in expenditure in SERPS over the 2000 level. These bonds will become due for payment as the cost of SERPS reduces in the longer term.

A Pensions Corporation. The role of co-ordinating the drive to adequate universal pensions will be the task of a new membership-run Pensions Corporation administered by the contributors themselves. This body will also be responsible for revenue collected for the new state pension arrangements. This will be levied at 2 per cent on weekly income on £10 to £60 and 6 per cent on all other income up to the current Upper Earnings Level (UEL)from employees and at the same rates, but without the cut-off at the UEL from employers. If the government pays into this account a sum equal to the difference between the 2 per cent levied on all income between £10 and £60 a week for all workers and the full 6 per cent rate, the fund will have a substantial surplus (£2.0bn) which could be used to begin pension contributions for up to one million carers and for some disabled people. Here will be a clear element of redistribution of the pension scheme to ensure that eventually all workers are fully included.

A simplified pensions savings vehicle. A new tax savings account will be established against which savers will be able to draw tax allowances of up to £6000 savings each year. It will replace existing direct tax allowances to pension contributions. Other tax subsidies to pension schemes will remain in place, apart from the tax concession on lump-sum payments which will begin to be phased out ten years after the introduction of the reform. The payment of lump sums will still be permitted, but with no tax advantage attached.

A National Insurance Corporation. A mutually-owned National Insurance Corporation will be established to organise in the first instance a new care pension and a new unemployment insurance scheme. The aim is that, over time, all the National Insurance benefits will be recast and brought into the new scheme.

A new care pension. The National Insurance Corporation will be responsible for running a new care pension. Practically everyone now reaches retirement age, so it makes sense to have a system of compulsory savings rather than a system of insurance. The need for extensive care at the end of a person's life affects only about one in six of the population. This is a risk which should be insured against. The proposal is for a compulsory system run by the new corporation so that risks are spread and premiums are low. The pension will be paid to the person qualifying on medical grounds. Stage one of the reform will be to cover the costs of residential and nursing care. A rate of 3 per cent on the new insurance base would be charged on all eligible income (reduced to 2 per cent on earnings below £60). This is estimated to be adequate to provide for costs of about £9bn, which is a reasonable target level for the cost of the first phase. (Note that this would also cover the Unemployment Insurance below.) If the charge is split equally between employees and their employers the rate becomes 1.5 per cent. If what is called the 'hotel charge' is taken from the total costs then the rate falls to about 1 per cent for both employee and employer. The Insurance Proposals have therefore been entered at a rate of 3 per cent on the new insurance tax base. This 3 per cent insurance charge will be offset by a cut of about 4p in the standard rate of tax, or other tax changes of an equivalent value. Stage two of the reform will be to allow the care pension to be drawn by people who qualify for help but prefer to remain in their own homes.

A new unemployment insurance. Unemployment insurance, like the Jobseekers Allowance which it will replace, will run for six months. In contrast with the Jobseekers Allowance, which relies heavily on sanctions against the unemployed, the new benefit will also be built on incentives. To match the changed job market, where pay for starting jobs has fallen and where many jobs have a short shelf-life, workers will bring themselves back into benefit eligibility after only thirteen weeks in work. The current rule which generally stipulates two years of contributions before benefit rights are restored militate against risk-taking. This benefit change aims therefore at sharing out new jobs more fairly between those households where no members currently work and those households where two or more members work. By weighting the benefit system heavily towards getting people back into work as quickly as possible - even on low rates of pay - the reform will help keep wives in work and thereby increase total household income. The cost of this reform is calculated by the Government Actuary at a 0.15 per cent increase on the new National Insurance tax and is included in the rate for Care Pensions above. This extra cost will be offset by a reduction in means-tested benefit costs. It is also expected that unemployment will fall as a result of this proposal.

The residual insurance system. During the first stage, the present system of national insurance, taxation will run alongside the new system, collecting at rates of 4 per cent (split evenly between employees and employers) for those insurance benefits not covered by expenditure for the new system. The cost of sickness, widow's benefit and incapacity benefit as well as the run-off of SERPS will be met in this way.

A proactive income support system. While these insurance reforms are designed to achieve universal coverage they also assume that people will take a greater responsibility for their own welfare. This change in the tenor of the welfare state fits the changing mood in the country and is in any case required to tackle the growing dependency culture which the Government's means-tested strategy has imposed on up to a third of total households. In order again to change the way people react and respond it is proposed to transform income support from a passive into a proactive agency. In place of today's deadweight budget, the huge income support payments will become an investment budget helping claimants to acquire education and training qualifications. All claimants below retirement age will be expected to consider how they can use the income support payments to help them move back into the labour market. Instead of being faced with the only option of working the system, claimants will have the opportunity of working themselves off benefit without being penalised.

INSTITUTE
OF COMMUNITY
STUDIES

18 Victoria Park Square, Bethnal Green, London E2 9PF
Telephone 0181-980 6263   Fax 0181-981 6719
e-mail: institute@commstud.demon.co.uk

WITH COMPLIMENTS

I: THE HIGH POLITICS OF WELFARE

The importance of welfare in the political debate has varied dramatically over the last two centuries. The early Victorian political settlement, coming as it did with the repeal of the Corn Laws and the passing of the Bank Charter Act, took most commercial and monetary questions out of party debate. The implementation of the new Poor Law similarly settled social policy.

This consensus was overturned largely by the efforts of Joseph Chamberlain. His 'unauthorised programme' doubly holed the status quo below the water-line. The Peelite view that Opposition should not put forward a programme until it had been 'called in' was directly confronted. Following hard on the heels of this challenge came another Chamberlain broadside. Fiscal policy ceased to be a matter of raising the necessary revenue with the minimum disturbance to private interest. Redistribution entered into the political fray. Welfare was again set on a course for high politics.

The Chamberlain challenge was one which Gladstone appeared only too anxious to counter, but his opposition brought devastating electoral consequences for the old Liberal party. A new welfare settlement had to await the Liberal landslide of 1906, and the use to which Lloyd George and Churchill put this overwhelming majority. New Liberalism's attempt to forge a sustaining coalition of voters again signalled a new high-water mark in the politics of welfare.

Welfare is set once again to become **the** issue of high politics. A new political settlement is falling into place over the political landscape. The collapse of the Berlin Wall and the cross-party agreement on the priority given to controlling inflation have largely removed foreign affairs and the running of the economy from the day-to-day battle of party politics. Welfare is thereby sucked into the centre of this political vacuum.

Welfare would have eventually taken that premier position anyway as the post-war settlement breaks down. The pressures fracturing the old welfare consensus come from a budget which:
- appears out of control
- undermines good government
- is increasingly destructive of honesty, effort, savings and thereby of self-improvement.

Each of these political pressures is considered in Section II. Yet even without such forces pushing welfare higher up the political agenda, the issue enters the major political league for a distinctly different reason. The self-imposed political innocence of the post-war political settlement, with its unspoken assumption of welfare's neutrality on character, now looks incredibly naive.

The largest single item in welfare's budget is pensions. Most of the budget therefore goes to individuals who have earned their entitlement, the payment of which has wholly beneficial effects. This is not true, however, of all of the welfare budget, and it is particularly not so of the fastest growing area of welfare - that of means-tested assistance. It is this part of the budget which goes largely to claimants of working age. Means-tests are the cancer within the welfare state, rotting decent values and overwhelming the honesty and dignity of recipients in almost equal proportions.

That welfare affects behaviour is not of concern only to recipients. It throws down an immediate challenge to would-be reformers. The age when contributors to the debate on reforming welfare can do so dispassionately, without detailing the values they wish to promote through welfare reform, should be brought to a swift end.

The beliefs and objectives underpinning **Making Welfare Work** and this volume are sevenfold:

- Welfare influences behaviour by the simple device of bestowing rewards (benefits) and allotting punishments (loss of benefits). With a third of central Government expenditure allocated by welfare, payments on this scale play an important part on setting down the general ground rules for society's behaviour. The nature of our character depends in part on the values which welfare fosters.

- Welfare should aim to maximise self-improvement, without which all is lost. Work, effort, savings and honesty must all be rewarded rather than, as so often at present, being penalised by welfare's provisions.

- Welfare has to reflect the pivotal role which self-interest plays within our motivations. Satisfying self-interest in ways which promote the common good should be a major objective of welfare policy.

- Welfare has to work with the changing labour market, giving people incentives and support to maximise their opportunities and thereby their rewards from work.

- Welfare should openly reward good behaviour and it should be used to enhance those roles which the country values. Those individuals who wish to buck the system and oppose the verities of civilised life should not be encouraged.

- Welfare should be given a central role guaranteeing universal citizenship in an age of stakeholder democracy.

- The aim of welfare's reconstruction therefore was to hold fast to the inclusiveness which was the central objective of post-war reforms, by offering new institutions popularly owned and controlled by the membership, which would win an enthusiasm from the majority.

These ideas, and a programme transforming today's welfare state, were put forward in **Making Welfare Work**. The following two sections summarise and add to the arguments which appeared in that volume. Section IV then takes the programme outlined in **Making Welfare Work**, develops it in terms of how it might be implemented, and includes the costings of these reforms made for this volume by the Government Actuary.

II: THE CENTRE CANNOT HOLD[1]

Key political assumptions

Making Welfare Work was based on five central political assumptions. The first was that the current welfare status quo cannot hold. Indeed, the surprise is that it has held for so long. In the current arrangements the poor are treated as inferior beings pushed increasingly on to means-tested assistance. Here lies the second political assumption. The disengagement from state welfare will continue with the poor being made increasingly vulnerable to second-class status. Only by seizing the initiative, by developing and offering a new welfare settlement which appeals strongly to the vast majority, might it be possible to secure for the poor full membership of the new welfare settlement.

The third assumption underscores the belief that welfare does not operate in a social vacuum. It influences character for good or ill. Because of the growing dominance of means-tests, welfare increasingly acts destructively, penalising effort, attacking savings and taxing honesty. The traditional cry that means-tests stigmatise is now a minor issue. They do for some, but this is simply no longer the main issue. Means-tests are steadily recruiting a nation of cheats and liars. Hence the urgency for reform. The responsibility for this appalling state of affairs rests primarily with this government which has made the extension of means-testing into a new religion.

But, fourthly, any new settlement will be dominated by the emerging values which prize ownership and control. What I have called the growing social autonomy of voters - wishing to do 'their own thing' determined on a basis of free association - will be the touchstone of the new welfare. The old-style corporatism of the state-run system either lies dead in the water, or awaits that fate. The futility of trying to resurrect the old order is the fifth political assumption which underpins **Making Welfare Work**.

1.   A pro-poor campaign

Social surveys have played a pivotal role in shaping Britain's social policy. At the turn of the century the 'condition of the people' was the issue - although it was dressed in a number of different disguises. The results of a whole series of social surveys came to dominate this debate: how many were poor; how best to help them?

Seebohm Rowntree was a key player in establishing who was poor. Rowntree defined poverty in such a way as to include the majority of the working class. The food component of Rowntree's calculations was by far and away the largest element in his poverty budget. The single observer to realise the full implication of what Rowntree had done was the statistician A L Bowley. As early as 1915 he observed 'the food ration used by Mr Rowntree as a minimum is more liberal... than that obtained by the majority of the working-class even in Europe in 1913, and by the great majority of the unskilled and agricultural labourers in England before the end of the fall of prices in 1895... it has come as a surprise to many people to learn what a large proportion of even an advanced population is insufficiently fed ... and that the poor and the working-class were really interchangeable terms in past generations'.[2] Working-class politics and programmes to help the poor naturally overlapped. Tackling poverty appealed to a huge constituency.

Bowley's comments referred to times past. While the interchangeability of the poor with much of the working class was still true at the time Bowley wrote, it became less so in the inter-war years. Steadily rising living standards for those in work was a marked feature of the 1920s and 1930s. It was those out of work who were set apart. In contrast, the post-war period of full employment ensured a steadily rising living standard for all those who wished to take work, which was plentifully available.

As the post-war boom faltered, and before the much more serious unemployment patterns of the 1970s and 1980s became what appear to be a permanent feature in the industrial landscape, a group of individuals, largely outside the labour market, was left untouched by the general increase in living standards. A new age dawned. The poor, as a group, were no longer identical with the working class, but were becoming distinct as differences in living standards cut them off from the mainstream of working class families. Hence the start of Britain's anti-poverty programme which targeted help on the poor only.

I do not believe there is public support for continuing a programme aimed only at eradicating poverty. Moreover, even if there were such a coalition in the

5

making I would argue against its mobilisation. Anti-poverty strategies until now have not merely failed, but have actually entrenched the poor even more firmly within their ghettos.

Here was the starting point of **Making Welfare Work**. Could a raft of policies be produced which the majority of the electorate would back with such enthusiasm that its comprehensiveness - of including the poor in the good life - would also be bought?

The aim was that this enthusiasm would spring from:

*   building a welfare reconstruction which was imbued with the aspirations and values of the majority;
*   a programme offering to counter, as far as human action could, the vagaries of economic and social life;
*   turning on its head the approach from one of 'being done good to', to one of carving out one's own well being.

2.   Expenditure growth

There are other changes already affecting Britain which will ensure a remaking of welfare's compact. A number of mighty forces are beginning to draw up and aim their fire-power against the social security budget. Change will be forced on a number of fronts. First there is the impact of the sheer size and growth of the social security budget, from 23 per cent of government expenditure in 1979 to 31 per cent in 1996. Matching that growth has been its share of GDP; from 9 per cent in 1979 to almost 13 per cent by 1996.

No matter how it is measured, the social security budget is growing at an extraordinary rate. The Government has abandoned its aspiration to cut the budget in real terms. It now embraces only the more modest goal of limiting social security expenditure's advance to below the underlying growth rate in the economy. The current claims by the Secretary of State to have reduced the annual growth and set it on a path below the underlying growth rate of the economy must be set against his own record, let alone that of the whole Government since 1979. During the period of Peter Lilley's stewardship the social security budget has each year burst through the annual increase agreed for it by the Cabinet in its annual public expenditure round by at least £1bn and usually by £3bn.

3. The undermining of good government

An attack on the social security budget has also opened up on a second front. Its inexorable growth is preventing good government. Since 1992-3 public expenditure has grown by £43bn. Of this increase, the social security programme, which already claimed the largest share of the total budget, cornered the lion's share of the increase, or two-fifths of the total rise in Government spending. In other words the largest budget is growing faster than any of the other major areas of public expenditure. The sheer size and the apparent uncontrollability of the largest of public budgets makes it increasingly difficult for the Government to prioritise expenditure over the range of its total programme. Aneurin Bevan once claimed that socialism is the language of priorities. Priorities are certainly the basis of good government. Over the past 17 years in particular, Cabinet Ministers have been taken prisoner by the imperial guard at the DSS whose overspend increasingly limits the ability of other ministers to take independent action.

4. More for less

The third force challenging the rise of social security expenditure stems from nothing less than a double paradox. Over wide tracts of public expenditure the Government has introduced market-orientated reforms. Their aim was not only to gain better value for money, but for those gains to cover the cost of any likely increase in demand for services. But Nicholas Bosanquet argues in his Social Market Foundation Publication, **Public Spending into the Millennium**[3], the impact of the reforms has been such, and the performance of parts of the public sector so enhanced, that the reforms themselves have created new swathes of demand. The reforms have therefore had the opposite effect to what the Government intended.

The second, and associated, paradox concerns how any increase in the supply of public goods can be paid for. Whether or not it is a true reflection, practically all senior politicians believe that to suggest a generalised rise in direct taxation would court electoral disaster. Apart from printing money or borrowing, moves which would be immediately punished by the international capital markets, only indirect taxation is available for such financing. Here then is the second and linked paradox. Demands for an increase in public expenditure are most easily voiced by middle-class groups, those with sharp elbows, anxious to get themselves and their families to the top of the queue. The most expedient political way of paying for those increases is by indirect taxation which bears most heavily on poorer people. Increases in public expenditure paid for by poorer groups but disproportionately benefiting richer groups is hardly a strategy a future radical government can contemplate with ease.

5.   Tory means-test strategy

At the heart of this Government's strategy to control social security expenditure is a grotesque misunderstanding of welfare's dynamics; herein lies the fourth force which has already begun destroying the beliefs which underpin the post-war welfare settlement. Tory Governments since 1979 have made the targeting of benefits the major means by which growth in the social security budget is controlled. That targeting has overwhelmingly assumed the form of means-testing. The Government's view is that these benefits provide the final safety-net in the welfare state. The reduction or abolition of insurance benefits saves money and anyone then left without adequate resources of their own will be eligible for means-tested assistance.

The post-war welfare settlement envisaged that means-tests would have a place in the new scheme of things. But their role was only ever meant to be a residual one. The intention was that, as individuals became eligible for National Insurance benefits, the numbers claiming means-tested benefits would fall.

The opposite has occurred. There are three main classes of benefits. The cost of contributory benefits since 1979 has increased by less than 30 per cent. Expenditure on non-means-tested and non-contributory benefits has risen by a little over 100 per cent. Expenditure on means-tested welfare however has rocketed, by almost 300 per cent in 16 years, ie ten times more than the increased expenditure in insurance benefits.

Table 1: Percentage increases in benefit expenditure between 1978/9 and 1994/5

[1] contributory benefits	28.5
[2] non-contributory benefits	105.1
[3] means tests	286.3

Source: House of Commons Library Statistical Section

In 1949 means-tested benefits accounted for one tenth of social security expenditure. By 1992 they accounted for around a third. With means-tested expenditure rising at this rate no-one should be surprised that, on the Government's own calculations - and correcting those I gave in **Making Welfare Work** - a third of the population lives in households which draw at least one of the major means-tested benefits - Income Support (IS), Housing Benefit (HB), Council Tax Benefit (CTB), or Family Credit (FC). Since 1979 this proportion has doubled.

These figures suggest that expenditure on means-tested welfare is out of control. But the extraordinary fact is that increasing welfare expenditure in this area has been a deliberate plan by the government as part of its strategy to cut the welfare bill. Why has the opposite of what was intended actually happened?

6.   Failure of means-test strategy

Means-tests do not operate in a vacuum. It is the way in which the eligibility rules for such benefits interact with human character which creates today's welfare disaster. If eligibility for a benefit is determined primarily on the grounds that income or capital is below a statutory level, then a penalty is imposed on honesty, effort and savings. In short, means-tests:

- cripple incentives - as income from work rises, means-tests bite and benefit value falls;
- penalise savings - people who save are likely to make themselves ineligible for benefits;
- tax honesty - those who are honest about their earnings and savings make themselves ineligible for benefit.

It is here that the Government stands doubly charged with naivety. They have ignored the way means-tests are eroding the values of work, effort, savings and honesty. How long can a society survive once these values are so determinedly undermined in the way that means-tests do? But this naivety about how human motivation will respond to incentives and disincentives is compounded by the Government's expectation of how the spread of means-tests will help control the social security budget. Far from limiting claims, each £1 of means-tested benefit helps generate the next £1 claim of benefit.

The National Insurance scheme has been cut back and increasing numbers pushed on to means-tested assistance. The government claims that this strategy saves money, ie fewer people are able to claim benefit. This would be true providing there are no perverse effects. The evidence suggests otherwise.

- The Government's view on the impact of benefits is totally static, ie what is the impact now on whether or not people claim benefit? Yet people's lives are dynamic, with their circumstances regularly changing. Most partners of unemployed men, for example, give up work when their partner ceases to claim National Insurance unemployment pay. The reason for this is quite simple. Once the unemployed person is forced to draw income support, the other partner's income is taken into account. So one office records a fall in the cost of unemployment benefit as a claimant ceases to be eligible. Simultaneously, but unrecognised by the government's data processing, the same claimant is opening a new account for income support not merely for himself, but often for his family as well.

- While one partner remains working, the unemployed partner is looking for a job that pays more than unemployment pay. Once both partners are unemployed the position is transformed. As the likelihood is that only one partner is going to gain a job - at least in the short term - that partner is looking for a wage packet which meets the benefit payments of at least two people. The job search is then confined to employment offering more than the tax free benefit level for an entire household.

- Once both partners are unemployed it becomes increasingly difficult for either to re-enter the jobs market, even if jobs are available. Means-tests operate like a vice locking both partners into long-term unemployment and thereby play a crucial role in the emergence of the two-wage-earner/ no-wage-earner syndrome.

- Means-tests also put a claimant's honesty on the rack. Should someone gain a full-time job they are likely to become ineligible for income support (though they may be eligible for family credit if they have children). Housing benefit is progressively withdrawn as income rises. So too is council tax benefit. Not surprisingly, therefore, a significant group of claimants fails to declare its earnings from work. A growing army of people now regularly cheats their fellow-citizens by claiming benefit while working.

- In this way means-tests act as the enemy within the welfare state, undermining honesty, work incentives, savings and effort. They also have a ripple effect on the wider society.

Once dishonesty has entered the system - as it now has on a massive scale - means-tests help perpetuate and expand claims. The key assumption about social security take-up is that people cease claiming when their need ceases, ie. when they are no longer unemployed or sick. Means-tests positively encourage claimants not to cease claiming, ie they penalise work in that the income from benefit is now above the wages of those jobs which claimants with families can realistically expect to gain. Moreover, means-tests encourage people to commit fraud, and once people are claiming fraudulently, fraudulent claims do not usually come to a natural end until the fraud is exposed. This pattern of fraudulent behaviour applies to individual claimants, to landlords and their agents, some of whom have turned housing benefit into a personal merchant bank, and groups of individuals who are best characterised as a new cult of serious criminal fraudsters.

In addition, considerable numbers of individuals know that the National Insurance system has no foolproof means of checking bogus claims - by the person using either their own number (if they are very simple), the number of someone else, or the number of a person who does not exist. Large numbers of people who are working are also claiming National Insurance benefits, housing benefit, or income support.

Once this dishonesty becomes endemic, the welfare state becomes destabilised.

The welfare bills rise as more claimants become eligible while others continue to claim. The government cuts eligibility for non-means-tested benefits in order to rein back the welfare bill, and thereby forces more people on to means-tested assistance. So the total welfare bill rises yet again and the government returns to make further cuts ... and that is where the debate currently stands.

Means-tests ensure that claimants' energy is channelled into working the system rather than working themselves off welfare. It is in the way they have an impact on effort, savings and honesty that means-tests are the most potent recruiting sergeant there is for the dependency culture.

Herein lies a strange political paradox. Means-tests provide the nexus of the dependency culture against which the government so passionately rails. Yet this dependency culture is of the Government's own creation.

7.   Means-tests and the underclass

The underclass is as difficult to define as it is easy to recognise when confronted with it. The major cause is the collapse of full employment and particularly the radically transformed employment position of those with brawn and little developed intelligence. But welfare continues to play a part in both recruiting and solidifying the underclass.

We live in an age where both personal and societal activities are increasingly judged on relative rather than absolute criteria - if judged at all. Within this changed atmosphere we need to set the operation of welfare in respect to how it encourages, sanctions or condones individual actions.

Means-tests are of growing importance in today's Welfare State and now command a dominant role in the lives of the very poorest. Means-tests sanction inaction, non-saving and lying. These powerful messages, relayed through the system which gives basic income support to the poorest, play a part in cutting the poorest off from mainstream Britain. By undermining the character of the poor, means tests also create a fertile ground for the 'yob culture', which again is one of the underclass's distinguishing marks for many male members, and for some females as well. Crime and drugs, themselves often linked, need to be added. Indeed the underclass, at its strongest point, is fed by unemployment, the abuse of welfare, crime and drugs.

Labour's Opportunity

This dismal picture presents Labour with both a challenge and an opportunity.

- Increasingly welfare is being fashioned on to a means-tested basis.
- Means-tests are recruiting sergeants for the dependency welfare culture.
- Means-tests play a determining role in the creation and maintenance of an underclass.
- Means-tests promote values which undermine the kind of society Labour pioneers proclaimed.

The welfare debate presents the Opposition with two political openings. First, presumably no Labour Government will want to support the Peter Lilley strategy of controlling public expenditure by restricting access to benefit, throwing claimants off the rolls and continuing above all to subject ever more claimants to means-tested assistance. An alternative to the Lilley strategy is urgently required. But an even greater prize awaits Labour. For, secondly, this area offers a golden opportunity to present a programme of welfare reform relevant to the new millennium which also re-establishes Labour's historic values in the centre of the political debate. At a time when it is alleged that Labour activists are unsettled by the pace of change within the Party, welfare offers the leadership the chance to demonstrate how it is keeping faith with Labour's historic mission.

What is fundamental is to ensure that the values which the Party was created to promote become central to a Labour Government's programme. In no area are those values more important than in welfare, and in no other area is the Party offered such a clear opportunity of once again expressing what those values are.

Welfare offers one of those defining moments for New Labour. The market system is correctly embraced in the running of the economy; welfare's reconstruction offers the chance to redefine what the Party means by the public domain in a totally new way from that in which it has traditionally been viewed in the post-war world. The principles on which Labour was founded - universalism, co-operation and mutual aid - would be central.

The welfare debate is also of first-rank importance in two other respects. No Government can remain neutral over by far and away the largest Whitehall budget. There are 21 Government Departments represented in the Cabinet. The Secretary of State for Social Security's budget is greater than the combined budgets of 18 of his colleagues sitting beside him at Cabinet meetings. How Labour approaches welfare will give the electorate a firm idea of the financial mettle and probity of a future Labour administration.

The following section outlines the assumptions which underlay **Making Welfare Work's** reconstruction programme. It then touches upon the social, economic and political changes which necessarily set the broad framework within which the politics of welfare reform have to take place.

III: RECONSTRUCTING WELFARE

Underlying assumptions

There are ten assumptions upon which **Making Welfare Work** built its reconstruction programme. **Making Welfare Work** argued that any reform of welfare which aims for a successful transformation must be one based upon:

- a balanced view of human nature
- greater contributor control
- comprehensive coverage
- key socio-economic changes
- the new social culture
- growing social autonomy and its relation to taxation
- the role of trust
- the decline in state power
- the belief in social progress
- new forms of social cohesion

1.   A balanced view of human nature

No welfare system can function effectively if it is not based on a realistic view of human nature. Self-interest, not altruism, is mankind's main driving force.

The view which exaggerated the place of altruism, and which was widely held by Labour activists during the latter part of the post-war period, was a far cry from the beliefs of the founders of the Labour Movement. The latter had a much more rounded view based upon a clear reading of human character. Mankind was (and is) capable of acts of extraordinary altruism, but altruism is generally secondary to self-interest.

To place self-interest at the centre of the discussion is not an amoral - let alone an immoral - act, as some of the Left seem to suggest by their response to **Making Welfare Work**. Nor has it anything at all to do with embracing Thatcherism. It is simply basing welfare policy on realistic assumptions.

Labour's failure to hold a balanced view of human nature presented a picture to the electorate of a party completely out of touch with reality. A party so short on street cred was simply unelectable. But while the distorted view Mrs Thatcher held of the aggressive, self-assertive side of human nature helped to win elections against a politically infantile Labour Party, the negative impact after 17 years of this total focus on self-interest is all around us to see.

A civilised existence often depends on striking the balance between opposing forces. To stress mankind's self-interest to the exclusion of all other attributes ensures that self-interest tumbles into selfishness; and selfishness can itself all too readily collapse into greed.

Part of the necessary moral order is not to do with decrying or thwarting self-interest, but with attempting to satisfy it in a way which is consistent with the public good. The most deadly charge which can be made against Britain's welfare state is that it increasingly ignores this cardinal principle. Welfare is instead pitted against self-interest in a way in which the public good can only be the loser. Hard work is penalised by the loss of entitlement. Incentives reinforce welfare dependency. Honesty is punished by a loss of income. It is in this sense that means-tested welfare is the enemy within. Its rules actively undermine the whole fabric of our character. In so doing it is a cancer within the public domain helping erode the wider moral order of society.

How should a rightly structured self-interest influence welfare reconstruction? **Making Welfare Work** argued for a stakeholders' welfare which would be increasingly insurance-based. Benefits would accordingly be much more closely linked to the payment of contributions and, with regard to pensions (far and away the largest area of expenditure), **Making Welfare Work** made the case for individuals owning their own capital.

Altruism has a clear role to play in the proposed reform. The structure would be made comprehensive by taxpayers paying the contributions of those people who were unavoidably out of the job market - through unemployment or because they were undertaking caring roles, for example. But **Making Welfare Work** was explicit in arguing that, for the time being, the age of large, unspecified redistributive acts was ended. Politicians who argue otherwise are a public menace.

I do believe, however, that hypothecated redistribution is possible within carefully defined parameters. **Making Welfare Work** attempted to define these limits. The redistribution has to be part of the scheme which the majority of the electorate supports for clear reasons of self-interest. Indeed, as **Making Welfare Work** argued, the altruistic element in the scheme had at least a flavour of self-interest about it, ie 'who knows which member of my family is going to lose their job again in the euphemistically named growing flexible labour market?' **Making a success of these welfare reforms, with altruism playing an important but subsidiary role, will open up the possibility of building on this altruistic element in further necessary reforms.**

2.   Greater contributor control

We live in an age of growing individual ownership, a development which has wide support from the electorate. A stakeholders' welfare state will be seen as part of this trend. It fits easily with the actual changes, which will be described shortly, whereby society is moving towards greater social autonomy.

I do not believe, moreover, that a reconstruction of welfare can take place on any other basis. **Welfare expenditure needs to increase in an age of growing demands for tax cuts. That expenditure will not be forthcoming under the existing rules. Voters will support schemes costing more only if they are their own schemes.** No-one now believes that the current National Insurance scheme is theirs, and that the future benefits they are currently paying for are safe. Taking unemployment benefit alone, while contributors have been asked to pay more, the earnings-related supplement to unemployment benefit has been abolished, the eligibility rules have been severely tightened, and, with the Jobseekers Allowance, the 12-month duration of benefit halved. A new National Insurance scheme controlled by the contributors must be established for voters to believe that their contributions will be safe and that the eligibility rules will not be changed against their interest.

Similarly, increased savings for pensions will be forthcoming only if these savings are individually owned. When old-age pensions, as they were called, were first introduced in 1908, payments were made only to the poorest pensioners aged 70 or over. That was at a time when the average male life expectancy was 48 years! Even after the latest government reforms on raising the retirement age for women qualifying for a retirement pension, the age of qualification will be 65, ie five years lower than it was in 1908. Yet this is not a time when only a minority of people reach retirement, and then live at best for a couple of years, as was the case in 1908. Today, practically everybody reaches retirement and lives on for one or two decades or more.

The bill to meet pensions can only be met by transferring a greater proportion of today's income to meet that cost. I do not believe that people will accept the transfer of income that is necessary unless the rules of the game are fundamentally changed. Hence the stakeholder principle, whereby each individual gains ownership over any new assets which are built up in the new scheme.

So, if the welfare debate is considered in traditional terms, and takes into account only levels of government expenditure, the total bill will indeed fall, and with it direct tax rates. But the aim of **Making Welfare Work** was to meet the welfare challenge in the early decades of the new millennium, and that can only be achieved if the amount of income spent on or saved for welfare increases. **But the key to acceptance of this great change is that the speed at which the reform is brought in will be an issue on which individuals themselves will have a say, the welfare institutions will be owned by the participants and the newly accumulated capital will be owned by them.**

3.   The role of comprehensiveness

The third principle underlying welfare reconstruction is that the new scheme must aim for comprehensiveness and that this objective must take priority over the level or value at which benefits are set. The significance of this reversal of priorities needs to be stressed. It amounts to no less than a sidestepping of a century-old tradition of British social reform which was touched upon in section II (**A pro-poor campaign**).

In **Making Welfare Work** the term comprehensive was meant to convey how the new welfare state should be inclusive, ie including all of the relevant groups and persons. This comprehensiveness was to take clear precedence over the level of benefit. **Making Welfare Work** rejected the idea of defining a poverty line and paying National Insurance benefits above this level which has been the traditional approach of the centre Left. I say 'approach' for it was never realised in Government.

Making Welfare Work's objective of ensuring that people are lifted free of means-tests also entails, in its initial stages, that the poor who are drawing means-tested assistance gain least from this strategy. For the traditionalist this approach is heresy; instead of delivering most help it delivers least to the poor who are already claiming. **Making Welfare Work** made plain that any successful disengagement from means-tests must inevitably result in this outcome; those drawing means-tested assistance will see no immediate increase in their standard of living, while others receive additional help as the new benefit structure begins to take effect. Here is another crunch point where it is vital that the reformer's nerve does not crack. This strategy offers the only realistic possibility of disengaging from means-tested welfare.

This emphasis on comprehensiveness breaks with the British tradition of social reform in a second important respect. The reconstruction of welfare along the lines of **Making Welfare Work** is **not** a readvocation of an exclusive state approach, ie providing National Insurance benefits valued at more than an arbitrarily defined poverty line. **The aim is to combine benefit provision with individual and household effort to ensure that living standards are adequate.** This change in direction begins to realign British social policy on a more clearly European line where this general underpinning of living standards is widely supported.

4.   Taking account of key socio-economic changes

The post-war welfare state was designed for a world where a full-time, fully employed male labour force brought home reasonable wage packets, where the traditional family model went unquestioned, where more women worked in the home rather than going out to work, where the overwhelming proportion of young people moved straight from school into work, where once a satisfactory job had been found it would last until retirement some 45 years later, and where retirement was itself of very limited duration.

The world has changed in a number of fundamental ways since the early post-war years, although these changes should not be exaggerated. A clear and accurate view of what has been happening in the labour market, within families and within the country's socio-economic culture needs to be reflected in welfare state changes.

- **Revolution in the jobs market**

There have been three changes in the composition of those in employment which have been billed as near-revolutionary transformations. First, for every woman turning up to work in 1948 there were two male colleagues. Less than 50 years later there were already more women than men working in some industries. Shortly there will be more women working overall.

A second near-revolutionary employment change has been the number of hours worked, and again a significant change occurred in the 1980s. Those in full-time work have maintained the length of their working week, yet the number of full-time jobs has dropped by almost three million. During the same period the number of part-time jobs has expanded by almost a third - or by just under two million.

The third change has been an increase in the number of jobs which make up what has been called the flexible job market, for it is in this part of the labour market that new or re-entrants have to seek employment. Three findings from the work of Paul Gregg and Jonathan Wadsworth[4] are central to the debate.

* Whilst in 1992-3 66 per cent of all work consisted of full-time permanent jobs, less than one third of new job placements were of this kind.

The marginal nature of these job openings is reflected in their pay. While the pay of those moving between jobs is clustered midway between half median and median weekly earnings, the pay of those entering or re-entering the labour market is skewed towards the bottom end of the pay hierarchy. For that group entering the job market the pay of 45 per cent was at a quarter of median aggregate earnings or less, ie less than £56 a week, while 55 per cent was below half median earnings.

* New entries into work generally gain less secure posts.

Over 50 per cent of employment inflows are into part-time or temporary employment. Such is the destination too of 65 per cent of those from non-employment. More significantly, only 14 per cent of those leaving full-time temporary work for permanent work are observed in similar full-time positions three months later.

*   The current system of welfare interacts with the labour market in a
    destructive manner.

Here we turn to the likely income from work for those on means-tested
assistance. Remember the Gregg and Wadsworth finding: 55 per cent of entry
jobs paid below half median earnings. The DSS estimates that, in 1991, a
couple with children on 75 per cent of median earnings could be gaining only 20
per cent more than their benefit income. Yet only 20 per cent of entry jobs paid
75 per cent of median wages.

With entry wages at this level it is not surprising that Paul Gregg and Jonathan
Wadsworth found that a significant change in the likelihood of gaining a job
depended upon whether one's partner was in work. In 1979 there was 'a positive
differential' in favour of unemployed workers finding work where their partners
were also not in work. When this analysis was carried out again in 1985 (and
in 1990 and 1993) the non-exit rate was reversed.

In 1979, even if both partners were unemployed, jobs were taken by one of the
partners which gained pay levels thought to be suitable in comparison to benefit
levels. Now the pay of entry jobs is such that the income from work for that one
partner gaining work is below - and often well below - the income of the
household from benefit. Hence the drive towards the two-or-more-wage-
households/no-wage-households. This is a crucial finding which we must take
into account when reconstructing welfare.

• **The growth in the number of single parents**

In 1971, when the only consistent series of data on single parents was initiated,
there were 570,000 single parents responsible for one million children.
Provisional estimates for 1992 indicate that the total has soared to 1.4 million
single parents - a near trebling in the space of a little over twenty years - who are
responsible for 2.3 million children.

The reason for this recent growth in the number of children in one-parent
families is due largely to the significant increase in the number of never-married
mothers. This is now the fastest-growing group of one-parent families - rising
from 90,000 in 1971 to 490,000 in 1992, an increase of 8 per cent a year.
Overwhelmingly these mothers are young and therefore could become part of

a growing group of single parents who are likely to have several children by different partners.

The growth of single-parent families should concern us for a number of reasons.

- Children of single parents are much more likely to be condemned to low income. Children of single parents account for less than one in five of all children. But these children account for very nearly two out of three - 1.8 million of the 3 million - children living on income support.

- More and more single parents are having to resort to means-tested income support. 43 per cent of single parents drew supplementary benefit in 1971. Today that proportion has risen to over 75 per cent.

- Single parenthood is the major cause of family poverty. Single parenthood now far outstrips unemployment as a cause of child poverty. One million single parents claim income support compared to just under 300,000 unemployed parents - less than 30 per cent of the numbers of single-parent families on benefit.

- We do not know the long-term effects for the 2.3 million children currently living without two parents.

How the income support system can be transformed from one which reinforces a single mother's separation from the labour market into one which becomes a proactive agency providing a life raft back into work, constitutes one of the major proposals for reform in **Making Welfare Work** and is detailed later.

- **New social culture**

While these are the main changes to the social and economic structure of Britain as they affect people, there is simultaneously a similar ferment in respect of ideas that individuals hold about themselves and the world around them, and these too bear directly on the direction which the reconstruction of welfare has to take if it is to meet with widespread public support.

In her DEMOS report **No Turning Back: generations and the genderquake**[5], Helen Wilkinson draws on survey work conducted by Synergy. Politics, including the politics of welfare, will be transformed in a society where the core values of authority, puritanism, security, well-being and connectedness are being replaced by risk, optimism, excitement, escapism and internationalism. And that is what this survey conducted over a twenty-year period shows. 18-to-34 year olds are likely to carry these values into middle age. New generations appear to be even more committed to these values and the life styles they embody.

How might these new values be categorised? Individualism, even positive individualism, simply has too much of a backward glance to it. Such a phrase also ignores the new wider networks based on friendship and love which are taking an increasingly central place in people's lives.

An emphasis on individualism also fails to convey both the richness and the geographical spread of many of the contacts which are now important to voters. A small survey[6] in the London Borough of Wandsworth, for example, revealed that, within the first seven months of 1994, 34 per cent of the sample had been abroad, 60 per cent kept in regular touch by telephone with personal friends or family abroad, and that of this sample, 31 per cent had lived abroad for part of their lives.

Welfare's reconstruction therefore needs to reflect this trend which I can best describe as social autonomy - social because life is very much seen in terms of one's relationships with others - in marriage, partnership and friendship - and autonomous because individuals increasingly want to decide matters themselves. This growing social autonomy is having an impact on - traditionalists would say fracturing - people' s attitude to the level of taxation. Both social attitudes and the developments in the economy are giving rise to greater choice.

5. Social autonomy and taxation

These two forces are coming together over the question of funding government activities. Economic changes have brought about a shift not only in the type of job, but in the manner in which people are paid. This itself allows more and more individuals a say in how and where they pay taxes, if at all. Two clear forces are at work which limit the scope of government to levy and collect taxes.

An ever-growing army of individuals is able to determine their tax rates over and above the simple choice of deciding what their income will be in any tax year.

The very highest earners now have the opportunity to move much of their income out of reach of the taxing authorities, either by creating tax frameworks which minimise their tax liability in their country of origin, or by choosing the most favourable tax regime elsewhere. This reaction by those who corner an increasing share of income is matched by those lower down the income hierarchy. While it is impossible to gauge accurately, the black economy is not merely alive but flourishing.

We are still living through an era when taxes are paid more or less quiescently, because the gains in education, health, and welfare far outweigh what could be purchased individually. The demand is not for root-and-branch dismantling of public services. It is more subtle than that. There is, however, a two-fold response to the continual rise in living standards, and a growing choice which both it and technological advances offer.

There is a growing demand for a say in the provision of public services which would have struck politicians as late as the 1970s as a mark of near-insolence in voters. The age of the *castrati* electorate is fast coming to an end. Here the Tories have caught the direction of the public mood. Indeed, all good left-wingers who support public services ought to be 100 per cent behind rather than mocking the Prime Minister in his drive for public-sector consumer charters. Without this move the force of the second change - the collapse of tax quiescence - will be even quicker and stronger.

As living standards continue to rise voters will want to spend for themselves the gains of increased earnings. This is one of the great forces for change which has all the appearances of growing in importance as time advances.

This drive towards greater individual consumer sovereignty is everywhere to be seen. Michael Young, the person most perceptive of new social trends, has written wittily of how what I have called social individualism functions in strong traditional families.[7]

He reports parents becoming reduced to the role of chauffeurs, motoring their children to individually chosen leisure pursuits, the children sitting alone in the back of a car listening privately to their own portable CDs or Walkmans, rushing up to their own rooms on returning home to continue playing with their computer games, appearing only at intervals to put food into the microwave, to eat alone before returning to the latest phase of their computer game or conversing silently with faceless names on the Internet. It is not only the pressure on building costs which has led to something like a third of all newly built homes having no place where a family could sit down together and eat a meal; there is simply less demand for such an outmoded use of space. This social individualism is also having an impact on how we regard our duties across the generations.

6. Social autonomy, taxation and welfare reform

Growing social autonomy and a changing view on the payment of income tax come together over the reform of welfare. The current view on tax rates places a major limit on welfare's reconstruction. It acts like an iron corset constraining attempts to change the status quo within a framework of common services. At this point it is important to pick up a theme which was touched upon in the Introduction.

Just as societies hold common stories about the past which help give shape to their current identity, institutions hold a double role other than their current utility. They forge a link with the past and offer a passage to the future. In addition some institutions play the role that ideals play in individual lives. And just as for individuals who are aware that the finest of ideals often remain at best only a partial influence on any part of an endeavour, so, too, societies have an equally pragmatic view about the functioning of institutions embodying a country's idealism. Most individuals would be affronted at being told that they had no ideals. Societies react similarly. And these common ideals are sometimes expressed specifically in institutions.

In Germany, for example, any government faces major difficulties if attempts are made to cut benefits. The social security framework is clearly part of Germany's public arrangements to which special protection is given. In Britain the status of the politically sacred has been bestowed on the NHS. The Nuffield war-time survey on Beveridge's proposals shows that ordinary voters most wanted the establishment of an NHS.

Why this should be is not easy to explain. A large number of older voters have clear recollections of being able to persuade a doctor to attend their sick children only if the money was presented first. Yet, similarly, large numbers of older voters were affected by poverty brought about by unemployment and low wages and imposed by the means-test. And yet the benefit system is not accorded the protection in our political culture that is bestowed on the NHS.

It is the idealised role the NHS has in British politics which is important for a major reconstruction of welfare. While a very small part of any National Insurance contribution goes to financing the NHS, the overwhelming part of the health budget comes from the Exchequer and is raised by a combination of taxes. The Government is reluctant to raise taxation to finance greater health expenditure and the public is wary of agreeing to the taxation without the certainty that it will be earmarked for health provision.

The proposal here is for a reconstructed National Insurance tax system to play a major part in NHS financing. The financing of health will be transformed. The Government will be able to ask the electorate the level at which they would like NHS expenditure to be set. A form of hypothecated tax for health care will be introduced which will have widespread support. The insurance ideal will not be reflected in the rights to treatment, which will remain in the hands of doctors. It will be in the knowledge that the payment of the insurance tax will result in finance for health services. At the same time the insurance tax will be used as the same basis for the reform of financing welfare insurance.

7.   Role of trust

An unspoken assumption about today's welfare state is that of trust. In a pay-as-you-go scheme, where today's contributors do not build up capital sums, but merely pay today's benefit bills, trust that future generations will do the decent thing and continue to pay, so that today's contributors can later draw benefits, is pivotal. Here then is a further great force making for change in financing welfare.

Changing attitudes to trust, and particularly to how it operates through generations, fix another framework within which welfare reconstruction has to be set. Far from taking this trust as given - as many left-wing reformers do - I believe we need to consider urgently how it can be supported and nurtured, while accepting that the growing push for greater social autonomy will lead to a re-evaluation of the role of trust in welfare.

The single biggest element of trust in today's Welfare State is given in the operation of the state's two retirement pension schemes. Today's contributors pay today's pensions in the expectation that their pensions will in turn be paid largely by an as yet unborn workforce.

Any serious politician would be cautious about placing too much financial pressure on this trust. It could simply fracture. This reason alone should lead Labour to reject ideas currently being put forward about rebuilding SERPS. To go down this route would mean that Labour is making promises to today's taxpayers which it will have no power to deliver from generations of taxpayers not yet born.

A SERPS approach has to be rejected for another reason. It typifies old Labour. Taxpayers are already showing signs of embracing additional pension costs. Very substantial numbers of workers are now covered by second pensions. The argument in **Making Welfare Work** was to make this trend universal by compulsion. What trust there is must be harnessed to help finance a new social security benefit for long-term care.

The demise of a world where trust was so taken for granted that it was never mentioned in public debate does not, unfortunately, complete the list of forces making for a fundamental rethink of Britain's politics. The role of the state is also being questioned.

8.   Decline of state power

Most of today's politicians grew up during those extraordinary years of the twentieth century - the decades of full employment following World War Two. Partly because there was full employment, but for other reasons too, there was a period of optimism about the power of the state. The nation state could, or at least could appear to, run the economy, and the state's writ ran throughout our lives; from birth, clinic, school, right up until we were safely delivered into the labour market where there was an abundance of jobs. It looked after us if for any extraordinary reason we were without a job. It also cared for us in old age.

The state no longer has the power to behave in a similarly omnipotent way today, particularly not in the most important of areas - that of jobs. In part this is because its legal writ no longer coincides so obviously with the structure of economic power and decision making - the internationalisation of companies and communications is increasingly reducing the effectiveness of nation-states. Financial deregulation, which has been taken much further here than in most countries, allows companies to operate across traditional geographical boundaries.

National governments will increasingly be made prisoners of these wider economic forces. Governments not only appear to be but indeed are helpless in areas of vital concern to their citizenry. Failure to perform effectively further undermines confidence in the state's power. The mechanics of decline are thereby definitely in motion. As governments look less and less powerful and effective, citizens will look elsewhere for services which previously were the province of nation-states. This change should not be over-emphasised. National governments have not been immobilised. But the direction of change is unmistakable. And welfare's reconstruction has to take note of this fundamental shift in the state's power and its ability to deliver.

Coinciding with this limiting of the national government's writ is perhaps an even more important revolution which has already been touched upon. Increasing numbers of voters no longer see the state as central in achieving the good life. Indeed, self-achievement is part and parcel of the good life. Consequently a growing proportion of voters now has a changed perception of what legitimately a state not only can but also should be expected to achieve. Rather than being the leading player, the state is increasingly cast in the role of an active umpire, setting rules and ensuring that fair play operates. This change alone could have major repercussions on any reform of welfare. But as we have seen it is only one of several forces determining the welfare agenda.

9.   Belief in social progress

By the end of the Victorian Age there was a widespread belief that, to use Sidney Webb's phrase about socialism, there was something 'inevitable' about social progress. The shock of finding that almost half of inner city dwellers volunteering for the Boer War were unfit for service merely renewed efforts at establishing a national minimum and thereby ensuring progress. Those balmy Edwardian days seemed to promise a continual summer with extension of the Empire overseas and progress at home. Four years' fighting in the mud of Flanders fields gave the first serious jolt to the idea that progress was inexorable and that it developed in an unremittingly linear fashion. The response, however, to the catastrophic events on the Western Front was for a renewal of effort. That surely was what was required, given the extent of the sacrifice in the trenches.

The idea that progress was not only possible, but was a duty to be pursued, underpinned the moral worth of the Attlee Government. And despite the fact that the electorate naturally, and only too eagerly, moved away from the austerity of the 1940s, the move was towards a society which was offering to spread consumer choice and rising living standards to the majority. Progress was again quickly seen as inevitable and its effect was expected to fall like God's gentle rain, uniformly over the entire population.

The Thatcher Government marks a break with this long tradition. Radical change there certainly was. But at the end of that near-permanent revolution the country is left with a marked cynicism about who has benefited from such change. The Thatcher years were marked by sweeping changes, but the benefits in terms of livings standards have been concentrated at the very uppermost reaches of the income pile. Progress is no longer seen to be a general movement embracing the whole population.

This has had an ironic political effect; while increasing numbers of people want to dissociate themselves from the Thatcher revolution, there is no great support yet for an alternative. There is widespread agreement about the need for change, but the change is presently more focused on personnel than policy.

Making Welfare Work sought to offer a raft of policies to reform welfare which might help direct this mood for change in a more positive direction. While one of the unspoken assumptions of the book was a reassertion in the belief in social progress, it was a carefully qualified one. It sought to learn the lessons that leading Edwardian reformers tried impress upon politics. Both left and right sought the mechanism which explained the startling social progress that was widely commented upon during the last years of the 19th century. The reformers designated the urge for self-improvement as the mainspring of advance and were anxious to ensure that any reforms supported rather than undermined this enabling force in mankind. **Making Welfare Work** debated how this lesson had been lost in the rush for welfare reforms and how best it might regain its pivotal position. It was for this reason that **Making Welfare Work** stressed the importance of welfare reforms being based upon an accurate and adequate understanding of human nature (commented upon earlier in this section).

10.   New forms of social cohesion

Societies need a common sense of identity, amongst other things, if they are to flourish. Historically this identity has usually arisen from the sharing of commonly-held stories about the past, the acceptance of the institutional framework which is the product of that common history, and a culture which, like these other attributes, changes over time, but does nevertheless hold together a cluster of core values.

In times of rapid change one of the roles of politics is to safeguard a community's sense of common identity. It is ironic that that objective is often best secured by not opposing change. The pace of change is possibly of even greater importance. But of much greater importance still, particularly at this juncture of British history, is for politicians to seek ways of reinforcing a sense of social cohesion without which society is in danger of fraying at the edges.

•   Breakdown of trust

The demise of the omnipotent state poses obvious dangers. Individuals, no matter how strong, cannot, in any numbers, survive by their own efforts. We are dependent upon unknown individuals fulfilling their obligations if our lives are not to be disrupted and made barren. This trust in unnamed and unknown individuals is fundamental. Once it begins to break down fault lines begin to open and society's fragmentation becomes cumulative.

Public trust has to exist within a wide span of activities of which tax and social security are but two. The more it is believed that tax evasion is on the increase, the more people will ponder the need for their own honesty. The more social security fraud goes unchecked, the greater is the possibility that others will 'chance their arm'. At the same time other taxpayers become more disillusioned with footing the bill.

This brings us back to the debate about the decline of state power, one facet of which we currently see as individuals stampede to look after themselves with 'the devil taking the hindmost'. These efforts to find new forms of safety and protection are as apparent in the welfare state as elsewhere. The collective provision by the state of second pensions for those outside occupational schemes has been ruptured as millions of policy-holders dive for personal pensions. That most of the contributions made to these pensions are modest in terms of building up pensions capital merely adds to the drama.

Some on the left have condemned the mass exodus from SERPS. But what to some left-wing eyes is a sign of selfishness is to others, with an equally left-wing vision, the only sensible course of action, given the current restraint on the options open to individuals. If there is a growing belief that future generations will be increasingly reluctant to meet the bills for a pay-as-you-go pension scheme, transferring into a funded scheme is not merely prudent. Not to do so is irresponsible.

- **Restoring confidence**

It was the lack of alternative welfare arrangements which would offer safety, while meeting the growing wish of individuals to have as a big a say as possible in how they run their own lives, which **Making Welfare Work** sought to address. **On offer is a reconstruction which gives individual ownership within a framework of commonly provided services.** Individual control is given in a way which does not harm others. Indeed, it offers them the same protection.

New institutional initiatives are urgently required to balance the growing wish of those paying the welfare bills to have a say in the ownership and operation of the schemes with the equally important requirement of maintaining the sense of common identity which the Coalition and Attlee Governments' welfare reforms instilled. The social security reforms proposed in **Making Welfare Work** aimed at strengthening the sense of social cohesion in our society while at the same time welcoming a move to greater individual ownership and control of the new common welfare institutions.

IV: MAKING A NEW WELFARE SETTLEMENT

Mechanics of Change

- **No consensus on welfare changes**

Making Welfare Work accepted that there was as yet no firm consensus on how to move determinedly away from the current Tory strategy. In this respect the politics of welfare reform is different from that inherited by Beveridge. While the Beveridge Report was an immediate bestseller, this success was not entirely due to Beveridge's intellectual, let alone his political, abilities. Two reasons above all others account for the impact his report had on the political debate. Its timing was fortuitous. Successes in North Africa suggested that perhaps, at long last, the war had begun to move decisively in the Allies' favour. Political eyes on the home front turned even more determinedly to the future.

There was, however, a second and perhaps more decisive reason for Beveridge's acclaim. From the 1930s onwards the work of Political and Economic Planning and other bodies produced a growing consensus on how welfare should be reformed. The Labour Party's proposals to the Beveridge Committee, for example, gave an outline which was not very different from the structure of the report itself.

Beveridge capitalised on and gave an enormous impetus to this growing consensus about what needed to be done. Today there is a similar agreement that reform is urgent. Voters know that the current system is brokenbacked; that far from combating poverty, means-tested welfare now constitutes a large part of the problem it is designed to fight.

There is therefore widespread agreement that more of the same courts disaster. What that change should be is now crucial. New directions can only come from political parties. Indeed, the acceptance by a major party of a clear programme to restructure welfare would help crystallise today's widespread unease into positive support for that very programme.

This approach has worked successfully before. In the build-up to the 1906 Liberal Government's welfare reforms there was a growing awareness that major changes to the Poor Law were necessary and desirable. There was no initial agreement on the nature of these reforms. In the end, the Government accepted and then reinforced the insurance principle which it inherited from the friendly society movement. This general approach as to the means by which welfare should be financed has been supported ever since by the electorate whenever it has been given the chance to choose.

National Insurance contributions are not viewed like a tax. Hence the absence of any outcry at the additional £27bn contribution since 1979 which has been accompanied by benefit cuts, and in some cases with their abolition. Similarly, that insurance contributions will be clearly hypothecated adds considerably to their appeal in an age when voters are reluctant to sign undesignated cheques over to the government.

Moreover the insurance base is the only financial basis by which reconstruction along the lines of a stakeholders' welfare can be meaningfully financed. Indeed it underscores the stakeholder principle itself. We will need to consider, however, whether this funding basis can 'take the strain' of the radically changed economic and social conditions of the last years of the twentieth century and function effectively as the years give way to the new millennium. The case for a stakeholder welfare system is also a means of strengthening a sense of social cohesion in society.

• **The key political commitments**

Building upon that concern for change must come from a party. The first crucial commitment from an incoming radical government is the phasing out of means-tested assistance's dominance. Such an objective cannot be achieved overnight. It will, in all probability, amount to a 20-year strategy. The proposal in **Making Welfare Work** was to achieve this end by phasing in a stakeholder welfare state.

This re-establishment of insurance-based welfare is not the traditional Left programme. In the past the emphasis of centre-left radicals has been on raising the relative value of insurance benefits so as to float claimants off means-tested support. Such an approach would be prohibitively expensive. It also ignores the role that human nature should play as an engine force within the welfare state.

An alternative strategy for freeing individuals from means-tested dependency is advocated here. The emphasis of **Making Welfare Work** was on establishing a near-universal insurance coverage and then harnessing self-interest to add to this insurance-based income. It is this universal coverage, so that self-interest can work within the law, with other family members free to work without fear of financial penalties being applied to the claimant's benefit, for which **Making Welfare Work** argued.

Two other commitments are also required. Large numbers of people will continue to rely on means-tests until stakeholders' welfare starts delivering. Single mothers, for example, will still draw income support after the reform is complete. It is crucial therefore to transform the income support machinery from a passive to an active body; from an agency which merely pays out benefit, and occasionally checks on fraud, to an agency supporting those claimants able and anxious to move back into the labour market to tailor their own exits from welfare.

The final commitment concerns striking a genuine partnership with the private sector. **Making Welfare Work** argued for a radical extension of the Left's concept of universal coverage. Up until now the Left has appeared to argue that only through a state system could universal coverage be achieved. In contradistinction, **Making Welfare Work**'s line was that the politics of welfare now makes it impossible for universal coverage to be gained through state provision. There simply is not the political support for such an approach.

The Left has to decide what is sacred in its approach. Is it the state-delivered element, or is it the guarantee of universal coverage which is the crucial ingredient? **Making Welfare Work** argued that the state-delivered element was a secondary issue to that of establishing schemes where everyone was a full member.

The proposals in **Making Welfare Work** were for a universalist approach to be applied through a mutually-owned National Insurance system, and through the private sector, in respect to pensions. The aim will be for everybody to be covered by the National Insurance pension and, in addition, for workers earning over £100 a week, in today's terms, to be members of an additional pension scheme. The case will be made here, however, that much of this new second or private pension could be provided more cheaply and safely under mutual-aid rules.

34

A transitional programme

The political commitment called for in the previous section forms the basis of a transitional programme. There is a fundamental need to move from the current welfare state, where individual effort is fatally undermined by the pernicious impact of an ever-expanding network of means-tests, to one which strikes a new partnership between collective provision - both state and mutually-aided - and individual effort. The three parts of this transitional programme are:

- universalisation of an insurance pension with membership of a stakeholders' pension scheme to run alongside;
- initiation of a stakeholders' insurance scheme beginning with care pensions and unemployment;
- recasting of income support as a proactive agency.

We need to look at what is entailed by each of these three reforms.

1.   A Stakeholders' Pension Scheme

Summary of the pension reform proposals

i.   **Ensuring every worker is entitled in their own right to a national insurance retirement pension.**

ii.   **Initiating a scheme of compulsory contributions to second pension provision for those workers who are earning above £100 a week and who are making no such provision at present.**

iii.   **Allowing savers to choose a private company or a mutually-aided body to which to entrust their own pension savings.**

iv.   **Closing SERPS from the millennium.**

v.   **Issuing bonds to cover the additional cost of SERPS entitlements over and above the current cost.**

vi.   **Establishing a National Savings Pension Scheme.**

vii.   **Establishing a National Pensions Corporation to spearhead the drive towards a universal pension coverage.**

viii.   **Establishing a new safe haven for long-term pension savings which will simplify both financial regulation and the current tax regime.**

ix.   **Encouraging mutual aid organisations.**

x.   **Bringing into pension coverage the first tranche of individuals**

currently outside the formal labour market.

Making pensions adequate

While the pension debate in this country has moved in a number of cycles, there has been one objective throughout. How can each of us be guaranteed an adequate pension in retirement? For **Making Welfare Work** it was this *aim* rather than the *means* of achieving this goal which was paramount. Here we examine how the debate has moved, from the extension of company schemes, to major state initiatives and then back again to the private sector with the advent of personal pensions. The debate has moved on once again. Attitudes are reshaping the political debate towards greater individual ownership and control. Economic forces are also at work pushing the choice towards a higher proportion of funded pensions. But before we consider the impact of this latest development, we need to look at what effect each of the past initiatives has had on pension provision. We will then be able to move to constructing a pensions audit.

- **Company initiatives**

The first initiative in providing pension schemes came from the private sector. By the early years of this century a few employers began to provide pensions for their workforce. By the outbreak of World War Two something like 2.5 million workers were covered by occupational pension schemes, or around 15 per cent of the working population. By the early post-war period, however, there were more occupational members in public-sector employment than there were in the private sector. That position had reversed by 1956, and by 1991, the date of the latest Government Actuary's report, six out of every ten workers gaining occupational pension coverage were in the private sector. Part of this change, of course, is due to the Government's privatisation measures, ie workers who previously had occupational coverage in the public sector are naturally classified as private-sector workers once their companies have been privatised.

- **State pension reforms**

Five major state post-war initiatives have been launched.

Boyd Carpenter reforms

Introduced in 1961, this reform marked the first acceptance by government that the state retirement pension was too low to prevent poverty, but that flat-rate benefits were too costly an instrument to remedy that poverty. Hence the search for an alternative which has dominated the debate ever since. The Boyd Carpenter reform was the first modest step towards earnings-related contributions and benefits.

Crossman reforms

It was not until late in the 1966 Parliament that Dick Crossman, then Social Services Secretary, announced that a national superannuation scheme would provide an earnings-related pension financed by earnings-related contributions. Occupational pension schemes which provided a set level of benefits could partially contract out of the new state scheme. The Bill incorporating these far-reaching reforms failed to complete its parliamentary passage before the 1970 General Election which Labour lost. The Bill therefore fell.

Joseph reforms

Sir Keith Joseph, as he was then titled, introduced the third major reform of state pensions. The plan was for a system of flat-rate basic state pensions financed by earnings-related contributions. An earnings-related component was to come from two sources. The main provision was to be through occupational pension schemes. Those who were not covered by an employer's scheme would be protected by a newly established State Reserve Scheme.

Castle reforms

Sir Keith Joseph had more luck - just - than did Dick Crossman in getting his scheme on to the statute book. The Act was due to come into operation on 6 April 1975. Before this date was reached, however, the Opposition had won the first of the two elections called in 1974. The newly elected Labour government announced that only the basic pension provision and the earnings-related contributions would come into force. In place of the main proposals Barbara Castle promised to combine the best parts of both the Crossman and Joseph reforms.

The result was the State Earnings Related Pensions Scheme (SERPS). Earnings-related contributions were to earn a flat-rate state retirement pension and an earnings-related additional pension. This would be provided either through SERPS or what was called a guaranteed minimum pension (GMP) through a contracted-out scheme.

SERPS is based on a pay-as-you-go principle. While this has considerable political advantages - such a scheme can come into immediate effect while holding out the prospect of a universal coverage of second pensions - the-pay-as-you go scheme on this scale left the scheme vulnerable at a time when the deliverability of intergenerational transfers through unfunded state schemes began to be questioned seriously for the first time.

SERPS, which opened its doors for business in 1978, marked the high-water mark of the dominant social tradition in Britain. It kept the state as the main player in providing the basic pension (where it was in a monopoly position), but as the major guarantor of the second earnings-related pension.

As well as envisaging a growing role for the state, the SERPS approach was the last pension measure which held out the objective of guaranteeing all pensioners an income above an arbitrarily defined poverty line. The other side of this goal, of course, was that of cost. It was on this point, more than at any other, that the two major parties divided once again on pension reform.

- **Fowler reconstruction**

A recasting of pension provision was one of the aims of the 1985 Social Security Act. Its purpose was twofold. It aimed at both:

- hauling back on the commitment future taxpayers would have to meet to run SERPS, and
- offering personal pensions as a more attractive alternative to state provision.

An underlying hope of the reform was to increase significantly the coverage of non-state second pension provision. To achieve this end two strategies were adopted.

The negative, or expelling factor, was to cut the value of SERPS entitlement. The second, positive approach, was to encourage membership of what were called for the first time personal pensions. Rebates and bonuses were offered to those who left the state scheme and took out a personal pension. Those who contracted into a personal pension plan were entitled to a 2 per cent contribution from the national insurance fund to their personal pension fund, over and above their rebated national insurance contribution.

The 1995 Social Security Act once again scaled down SERPS entitlements so that the cost (and benefits) of the scheme in 2040 will be half of what it would otherwise have been following the Fowler cuts.

The lessons

There are three lessons to be drawn from this thumbnail sketch of the post-war history of pension reform. First, good timing is clearly essential if a major welfare restructuring is to be successfully piloted on to the Statute Book. The move needs to begin soon after a General Election victory and not towards the end of a Parliament's life. A second lesson to be learned from these episodes is not the usual one on the need to forge a bipartisan approach. That clearly has attractions in that it offers immediately a political stability which is necessary if long-term savings are to prosper. But such an agreement was struck when SERPS was introduced only for that consensus to be broken by the Thatcher Government. **The only lasting long-term pension settlement is going to be won when the power of the saver is such that no political party risks incurring the wrath of this growing section of the electorate.** Hence the importance **Making Welfare Work** attached to the stakeholding principle in its own right, and as the surest way of offering cover for any short-term political flak. The third lesson to draw from all these efforts at instituting reform is that, despite second pension coverage, universalism has still a significant way to go. The extent of this pension shortfall is the subject to which we now turn.

Pensions audit

How successful have these strategies been in gaining universal coverage of second pensions? And how adequate are the contributions being paid towards securing a sufficient retirement income?

Definitions of adequacy must be, by their very nature, arbitrary. A proposed 16 per cent of salary is taken here as the target level at which to aim. The proposal is to phase in contributions over time to meet this target for all workers and for target groups outside the labour market. Many people, together with their employers, are already paying at this level. Occupational schemes, where charges and administrative costs are lower than in other schemes, are able to offer adequate pensions at a lower percentage salary and wage cost.

It is important to emphasise that there is no 'magic' contribution level which will guarantee an adequate retirement pension. The retirement income eventually provided by a set contribution level will depend on:

- the investment return achieved (best considered relative to earnings and/or prices in nominal amounts);
- the administrative cost (or charges, which may of course be different from the actual cost);
- the nature of the individual's work history, especially the number of years worked and also the level and pattern of earnings in those years; and
- the age at which the pension is paid (as it is highly geared to the expected duration of the pension) and, for money purchase schemes, the investment conditions when the pension savings are annuitised.

How many workers are already members of occupational or personal pension schemes paying contributions at around the 16 per cent level? And how many workers are paying only part of this size of contribution, or no such contribution at all?

Given the data which are available (and the necessary simplifications in the methodology) it was not possible for the Government Actuary to provide precise estimates of the number of workers by income levels who would be required to pay contributions - or greater contributions - to their pension scheme. Although data are available on the amounts paid into different types of pension provision it is not possible to combine all the different types and levels of provision in respect of individuals. What is possible is to provide estimates of the size of non- or partial coverage of occupational and personal pension schemes. This information is provided in the section below. Two further sets of information are then provided. The first looks at the increasing contributions required by employees paying no contributions to second non-SERPS pensions. Estimates are then provided for the total increase in contributions required from that group of workers who are currently making inadequate savings or none towards a second non-SERPS pension.

Occupational schemes

The Government Actuary reports regularly on the coverage of this form of pension provision. The latest report was for 1991 and the details of this form of pension coverage are given in the following table. In that year, 48 per cent of the employees were members of occupational schemes. This marks a fall from a peak level of coverage of 52 per cent which was recorded in 1983. The fall is due primarily to a combination of the decline in manufacturing industry and to the fact that new firms are less likely to offer occupational pension coverage than existing firms.

Occupational pension schemes overwhelmingly offer defined benefit pensions,

Table 2: Employees in pension schemes 1953-1991, United Kingdom (*millions*)

Year	Private sector		Public sector		Total members	Total employed	Percentage employed who are members		
	Men	*Women*	*Men*	*Women*			*Men*	*Women*	*Total*
1953	2.5	0.6	2.4	0.7	6.2	21.9	34	18	28
1956	3.5	0.8	2.9	0.8	8.0	22.7	43	21	35
1963	6.4	0.8	3.0	0.9	11.1	22.9	63	21	48
1967	6.8	1.3	3.1	1.0	12.2	23.2	66	28	53
1971	5.5	1.3	3.2	1.1	11.1	22.5	62	28	49
1975	4.9	1.1	3.7	1.7	11.4	23.1	63	30	49
1979	4.6	1.5	3.7	1.8	11.6	23.4	62	35	50
1983	4.4	1.4	3.4	1.9	11.1	21.1	64	37	52
1987	4.4	1.4	2.8	2.0	10.6	21.6	60	35	49
1991	4.5	2.0	2.3	1.9	10.7	22.5	57	37	48

The table excludes employees who have some pension scheme rights but are not accruing benefits in an occupational pension scheme in respect of current employement.

Sources for the numbers of scheme members: For 1953 the report of the Phillips Committee, subsequently, surveys by the Government Actuary.

Source: Government Actuary's Department 'Occupational Pension Schemes 1991 - Ninth survey by the Government Actuary'

ie pensions set at a proportion of final salary or wage levels. Of the 10.7 million employees who are members of occupational schemes, 9.8 million are in such schemes. It has been assumed for the purposes of the calculations underpinning the costs of the reconstruction programme that members in occupational schemes will be gaining benefit broadly equivalent to that which could be purchased by a contribution rate of 16 per cent throughout their lifetime. As a result it is assumed that the proposals would not result in extra contributions having to be paid in respect of members of defined benefit schemes. Of the 900,000 workers who are members of defined-contribution or money-purchase schemes, as they are sometimes called, (ie. the pension relates to the value of the capital amassed and the income derived therefrom - usually by way of an annuity), the size of the contributions paid by the members themselves is given in table 3.

Table 3: Numbers of members paying various contributions of salary to money purchase schemes *(thousands)*

Money Purchase Schemes	Private sector		Public sector	
	Contracted out	*Not contracted out*	*All*	*Total*
Under 2%	-	25	-	25
2% and under 3%	65	60	-	125
3% and under 4%	45	65	-	110
4% and under 5%	40	45	-	85
5% and under 6%	50	60	-	110
6% and under 7%	10	10	-	20
7% and over	20	10	-	30
Employee's share of NI contracted-out rebate	170	-	-	170
Total paying percentages	400	275	-	675
Non-contributory or other basis[1]	30	195	-	225
Totals	430	470	-	900

(1) Includes members whose contributions are purely voluntary

Source: Government Actuary's Department 'Occupational Pension Schemes 1991 - Ninth survey by the Government Actuary'

Other data (table 4) show there is a widespread range of employer contribution to money-purchase schemes, generally at a slightly higher level than that paid by the employee. In many of these schemes the contribution rates increase with age. Given the numbers in money purchase schemes and the levels of contribution already payable, the Government Actuary considers that the extra savings resulting from those schemes having to increase their joint contribution rates to the minimum required level would be relatively small and they have been ignored in the estimates. However some schemes would certainly have to amend their provisions.

Table 4: Number of members of private sector defined contribution schemes by employer's contributions payable *(thousands)*

Contribution basis	Contracted out	Not contracted out	Total
Under 4%	160	70	230
4% and under 6%	130	80	210
6% and under 8%	50	60	110
8% and under 10%	30	70	100
10% and over	50	70	120
Discretionary	10	120	130
Totals	430	470	900

Note
(1) It is estimated that there were about 170,000 members of contracted out money purchase schemes who were required to contribute only the minimum amount equal to the employee's share of the NI rebate.
Of these 170,000 members, 90,000 were in schemes in which the employer was only required to contribute the minimum amount, ie equal to the employer's share of the rebate.

Source: Government Actuary's Department 'Occupational Pension Schemes 1991 - Ninth survey by the Government Actuary'

Personal Pensions

The number of personal pension holders has grown rapidly since the introduction of personal pensions in July 1988. Four powerful incentives have been offered by the government to persuade people to take out such pension coverage. The schemes allow for the equivalent part of a person's National Insurance contribution equal to that of the rebate to be paid by the DSS to a nominated appropriate personal pension scheme. The tax relief on the employee's share of this rebate is also paid to the designated company, effectively increasing the rebate rate. In addition, a 2 per cent bonus was paid on top of this 5.8 per cent contribution. The general 2 per cent bonuses have now been recast into a subsidy weighted to older workers aimed at persuading them not to contract back into SERPS. Lastly, the capital funds into which these monies were transferred became the personal property of the employee. The attraction of these factors is seen in Table 5.

Table 5: Personal pension for employees: number of arrangements *(thousands)*

	1990/91	1991/92	1992/93	1993/94	1994/95
DSS rebates only	2,750	3,050	3,050	2,900	3,050
DSS+employee	1,400	1,450	1,550	1,500	1,650
DSS+employee+employer	500	650	1,000	1,150	1,300
Other	1,600	2,150	2,500	2,500	3,500
Free standing AVCs	250	400	600	650	800

Notes
(1) Figures for 1994/95 are provisional
(2) An individual may have more than one arrangement, so the figures neeed to be treated with caution.

Source: Inland Revenue Statistics, HMSO, 1995, Table 7.5.

There are no data available on the distribution of the level of contributions which are in payment to personal pension schemes. What information there is has been given in Table 5. The top three lines of the table are the key ones for our discussion. Of the 6 million members of appropriate (DSS) personal pension schemes in 1994-95, about one half pay no more into their personal savings scheme other than their rebates.

There are no official data on the distribution of other contributions. Some people - probably those nearest retirement - will be paying substantial contributions, perhaps right up to the Inland Revenue limit. What data there are come from the Inland Revenue and these suggest that only relatively small amounts are being paid in addition to the DSS rebates. The average contribution rate to personal pension schemes which are not connected to DSS rebates is only about 5 per cent of average salaries of those in such a scheme. In estimating the extra savings from requiring compulsory contributions from those not in occupational schemes, the Government Actuary reduced the total amount of required contributions payable by those not in occupational schemes by the amount currently paid towards personal pensions on the assumption that these would effectively be absorbed into the new requirements.

Pension coverage

Which groups are most likely to have gained inadequate pension coverage from these schemes? It is possible to look at the distribution by income and age of occupational and personal pension schemes. Current pension scheme membership by age and sex is given in Table 6 below. Here three remarkable trends are apparent, although it is important to add that these findings were constructed from a relatively small sample and, in addition, it is possible that some respondents misunderstood the question they were being asked. The coverage may therefore be an overestimate of the true position.

The first trend is the near total coverage of male employees during their peak years of economic activity - ranging from 90 per cent coverage for the 25-34-year-old worker group, to 99 per cent coverage for the 35-44 age group. For women working full time a not dissimilar trend is apparent, although at a somewhat lower level. Coverage here peaks at 83 per cent in the 35-44 age group of women workers. This group is likely to continue their pension coverage until retirement. Other things being equal, therefore, the pension coverage of full-time women workers will continue to improve. The third trend is for women working part-time who are least likely to gain occupational or private pension coverage. And yet amongst this group over a third of those aged 25-54 are in an occupational or personal pension scheme. SERPS coverage for the non-occupational or personal pension holders for all three groups of workers is considered in a moment.

Table 6: Percentage pension scheme membership by age and sex

	Age 18-24	25-34	35-44	45-54	55 and over	Total
Men full time						
Occupational pensions	30	55	68	72	62	60
Personal pensions	18	36	31	25	19	28
Any pension	49	90	99	97	81	88
Women full time						
Occupational pensions	30	53	62	62	62	53
Personal pensions	18	24	21	18	10	20
Any pension	48	77	83	80	72	73
Women part time						
Occupational pensions	1	23	23	22	15	19
Personal pensions	4	12	12	13	7	11
Any pension	5	35	36	35	23	30

Source: General Household Survey 1994, Table 8.1, HMSO, 1996.

Second pension coverage can also be classified by income group and data on this score are given in table 7 below.

Table 7: Percentage coverage of second pensions by income group

Pension scheme	Usual gross weekly earnings (£)						
	0.00 -100.00	100.01 -150.00	150.01 -200.00	200.01 -250.00	250.01 -300.00	300.01 or more	Total
Men							
Occupational	39	19	35	52	62	77	60
Personal	15	21	29	33	28	28	28
Women							
Occupational	20	19	47	66	68	77	53
Personal	16	20	21	18	20	23	20
Part-time women							
Occupational	9	41	38	50	[62]	[69]	19
Personal	8	16	20	16	[27]	[19]	11

Numbers in [ ] are derived from small numbers in the survey.

Source: General Household Survey 1994, Table 8.5, HMSO, 1996.

By knitting this information together with that from Table 6 it is possible to suggest which are the largest groups by income and age paying no contributions to occupational or personal pensions. Unsurprisingly, non-coverage is to be found overwhelmingly amongst the lowest income groups and, generally speaking, these groups are composed of younger workers, although a significant portion of older employees is not making extra provision. Part of any new initiative must therefore be to persuade workers to join pension schemes earlier than they currently do. The same trend is also observable for women working part-time, but the non-coverage is much more marked for the lowest income and youngest age groups. The figures in the table support the warning earlier that these data should be used cautiously as respondents may have sometimes misunderstood the question. For example, 104 per cent of men earning over £300 a week have second pension coverage!

SERPS

All those in employment, earning above what is called the lower earnings level for national insurance contributions (currently £61 a week) are required to be members of an occupational pension scheme or a personal pension scheme or to contribute to SERPS. The pension position of all those in work in 1978-79, when the SERPS scheme came into operation, and in 1992-93, is given in Table 8 below. This shows two trends which have already been commented upon: a decline in the numbers contracted out of SERPS due to membership of an occupational pension scheme and a very significant jump in contracting out by those workers moving into personal pension schemes.

Pensions deficit

More significant for the purposes of this discussion on the move towards universal coverage of second pension provision, are the data in the table relating to the self-employed and to those below the lower earnings level.

- ### Self-employed

There is a growth in the numbers of self-employed who are not members of SERPS, from 1.2 million to 1.9 million people. There are, unfortunately, no data on how many of this group are members in 1978-9 of what were termed '226 policies' and which have since been refashioned as personal pensions. The current position shows that around 1.1 million of the self-employed hold such policies but almost as many, 0.9 million, do not.

- **Below earnings threshold**

When SERPS was introduced, married women who paid what was called the married women's option (a much lower national insurance contribution offering only minimal insurance coverage in their own right) were allowed to continue with this contract. 3.6 million married women did just that. By 1992-3 the size of this group had declined to around half a million. In part this change occurred because a large number of women workers who opted for the lower national insurance contribution have now retired, and no newly employed married woman was allowed to opt into such status after 1978. But, also, the attitude of married women workers has undergone a significant change. Many more now see themselves as workers seeking full insurance coverage in their own right, and not as relying on their husbands' contribution record.

Table 8: Second pension coverage in 1978/79 and in 1992/93 *(millions)*

	1978/79	*1992/93*
SERPS	9.7	6.3
Personal pensions	-	5.7
Contracted out employees	8.6	7.8
Self employed	1.2	1.9
Mixture of contracted out and non contracted out	1.3	1.0
Voluntary contributions	-	0.1
Reduced contributions	3.6	0.5
Total number paying NI contributions	24.9	23.7
Below threshold	2.3	3.1

Source: House of Commons Library Statistical Section

This extension of the coverage of second pensions has been partially offset by a counter-trend; the number of workers earning less than the minimum income required for inclusion in the National Insurance scheme and thereby into SERPS. Again the figures are silent and do not tell us to what extent a number who previously would have opted for the married women's option now ensure they earn wages, perhaps from a number of jobs, each of which pays below the National Insurance contribution level. 2.25 million of a larger workforce in 1978-9 were paid wages below what is called the lower earnings level (LEL). By 1992-3 this total had risen to 3.1 million workers.

This trend is important for two reasons. Far from moving towards a universal provision of second pensions, this group has no such coverage in their own right even to the basic retirement pension. Equally worrying is the fact that the exclusion mechanism - the lower earnings level - has for the past 15 years been set as a declining proportion of average earnings. The lower earnings level is linked to the basic state retirement pension. Since 1980 this pension has been increased only in line with prices and not earnings. So the LEL itself has fallen relative to average earnings. Yet the numbers below this level have risen by about 40 per cent. Here then is another reflection of what has been happening to the earnings of the lowest-paid. The number earning under median and half median earnings has grown as a proportion of the total workforce, as the number of low paid jobs continues to advance.

In fact many of these workers are likely to qualify for the basic pension as a result of their home responsibility protection (women with children, for example, form the vast majority of part-time workers). No allowance has been made for any financial effect of bringing workers below the current lower earnings level into contribution liability and benefit expenditure. Although there would be a small net cost on pensions expenditure, those people currently earning below the LEL will make small National Insurance contributions and the relatively small amounts will broadly offset each other. These workers will make small National Insurance contributions and benefit entitlement will be gained in their own right.

- **Outside the labour market**

There are substantial numbers of people of working age who do not have jobs. Some of these economically inactive people have willingly retired early and have a substantial income from an occupational pension. Others have retired due to ill-health and draw invalidity benefit as well as an occupational pension. Currently there are 625,000 such claimants drawing on average an occupational pension of about £70 a week.[8] But many others are out of the labour market through no choice of their own and have no other major sources of income other than that which they derive from benefit. While these individuals will not currently be contributing to their pension funds, some, and maybe a substantial number, will have made contributions in the past and will, therefore, have frozen pension rights. There are four main groups currently excluded from the labour market; single parents, the unemployed, the sick and those caring for the long-term sick and disabled.

- **The total excluded**

A century after the introduction of the first company pension schemes, almost 20 years after the start of SERPS and 8 years from the countdown from personal pensions, a significant number of people have no right to an occupational or personal pension or to SERPS, and the size of this group is growing:
- 3.1 million workers paid no contribution into the National Insurance Scheme or SERPS due to their low earnings.
- Of the 1.9 million self-employed excluded from SERPS, only 50 per cent have personal pensions.
- A significant group is outside the labour market although its members are of working age.

Even greater numbers will have inadequate second pension coverage.

Some 4 million workers are currently making no contribution to a second pension scheme and most are registering no entitlement to the state's basic pension. Some of this group of 4 million may have paid contributions in the past and may gain some provision through their husband's or partner's entitlement, or may have entitlement enhanced by home responsibility protection. That will not be true of all.

This picture however underestimates the size of this vulnerable group. To the 4 million total we need to add those individuals who are making inadequate pension contributions. The group is heavily, although not exclusively, concentrated in the personal pension sector.

These figures point to one clear conclusion. Despite the welcome advance of funded pension provision, and of SERPS, the present pension arrangements for guaranteeing second pension coverage are leaving a significant proportion of the population vulnerable in old age. New initiatives are required.

Pension Reform One

The first move in gaining adequate pension cover is for every worker to be included in the National Insurance scheme so that they qualify for a National Insurance pension in their own right. Everybody earning over £10 a week will be required to

contribute to the new National Insurance Fund run by the Insurance Corporation. Earnings from £10 to £60 a week will attract a 2 per cent levy from employees, employers and the self-employed. Those earning above £60 will contribute 6 per cent on all earnings above that level up to the UEL; their employers will pay 6 per cent on all earnings over £60. This puts in place the first building block for an adequate retirement income, ie set at a high proportion of previous earnings.

Pension Reform Two

Workers earning above £100 weekly and not already contributing to a second pension will be required to do so.

• **The Lilley strategy**

The main opponent of this strategy is Peter Lilley, the Social Security Secretary. What is the basis of the Secretary of State's opposition to the idea of compulsory contributions for workers earning over £100 a week?

The Secretary of State presents his strategy as one based on the voluntary principle. But it is, of course, nothing of the kind. Workers earning above the LEL have always had to contribute towards their National Insurance pension. Since the advent of SERPS such workers have also had to make payments into SERPS, into occupational or into personal pension schemes.

Making Welfare Work argued that the Lilley approach was not adequate and that to some extent we now have the worst of both worlds. It is neither a voluntary policy, nor does it deliver the full advantages which should stem from a comprehensive compulsory policy. It is only a voluntary policy in respect to those who do not make any pension savings and it is this group which is the problem. The current compulsory policy leaves a significant, and perhaps a growing, total of people outside either SERPS, occupational or private pensions. Large numbers of those people who have opted out of SERPS - or out of their company occupational scheme - pay inadequate contributions into their own pension fund. Many of these workers, and even larger numbers of those paying

51

no pension contributions at all, will be drawing means-tested welfare in retirement. Moreover, all those groups outside the labour market are currently making no pension contributions.

Support for compulsion

Support for a comprehensive compulsory approach to second pension provision has quickly gained ground since Matthew Owen and I published our proposals in 1993.[9] The Commissions established by the Labour and Liberal Democrat Parties have subsequently come on board.

- Labour's Social Justice Commission[10] was lobbied to give support to the idea of compulsion. In its report the Commission backed this approach as one way of advance. As the Commission's other proposal was to advocate a re-adoption of SERPS, now seen by most people as a non-runner, compulsory provision was the Commission's only workable proposal.

- The Dahrendorf Commission on Wealth Creation and Social Cohesion[11] unequivocally backed compulsion as not only a preferable approach to increased taxation, but as advancing in a concrete form the idea of extending stakeholding.

Other influential bodies too are now lined up behind a comprehensive compulsory savings proposal. The World Bank's **Averting The Old Age Crisis**[12] saw the mandatory approach as advancing both efficiency and growth. The National Association of Pension Funds has more recently backed a proposal to make contributions to a second pension compulsory. The independent Retirement Income Commission[13] has given similar support.

A groundswell in favour of compulsory second pension provision is already developing amongst voters and is pinpointed, for example, in a survey conducted by NatWest and published in September 1995. This reported that 55 per cent of working people now believe it is up to individuals to provide for their own retirement. Of the two options - increased taxation or compulsory savings - 48 per cent of those questioned already favoured that of compulsory savings. The proposal in **Making Welfare Work** was not of course the scrapping of the state retirement pension scheme - which the question in the NatWest survey seemed to assume - but of ensuring that every individual in retirement would be drawing income from at least two pension schemes, the one provided by the state and that organised under the compulsory savings proposals.

Even greater support for new forms of welfare was recorded in a survey conducted recently by Coopers and Lybrand. Respondents felt that the recession had permanently affected their attitudes and that they could not rely on the Government to provide for them in either sickness or old age. 87 per cent strongly agreed with the proposition that 'you cannot count on the government - you have to look after yourself'. How can this clear reading by voters of the likely welfare state development be harnessed into an effective strategy? And, more immediately, what is going to be the response of the Government?

Against extending compulsion

The policy of extending compulsion - a key recommendation in **Making Welfare Work** - is attacked as no more than a hidden tax increase. That, as Peter Lilley claimed in his February 1996 Politeia Lecture, 'it may not *be* a tax increase, but it would feel like a tax increase. Labour should confess that their proposals would mean fewer pounds in people's pockets'.[14]

As ever, Peter Lilley chooses his words with great care. He does not attack the principle of compulsory savings - how could he, given that it underpins the existing National Insurance system, and SERPS, and is most people's understanding of occupational pension schemes? Instead, playing on the very breakdown of trust which was discussed earlier, he adeptly raises in people's minds the threat that any funds *saved* through a state-imposed compulsory scheme would be *imperilled* by the threat of the same kind of wipe-out that has afflicted a generation of SERPS contributors, and which has been carried out by his government.

It is exactly for this reason that **Making Welfare Work** was insistent upon the new Stakeholders' Corporations being statutory bodies independent of the government. There is no question of 'fewer pounds in people's pockets': just the same pounds in people's pockets, but at the time in their lives when they need them most - the principle underpinning savings throughout the ages. A government *could* seek to expropriate the funds of the new corporations, just as it *could* seek to sell Buckingham Palace. But the new Insurance Corporation (see below) is a holding body setting rates of benefits and contributions and budgeting on a yearly basis. There will therefore be no build-up of funds for a government to raid. Moreover, the annual budget and the funds thereof will be in the hands of the contributors - both employer and employees - themselves.

There will be new pension funds resulting from the universalisation of provision. But these funds are not held, let alone owned, by the Pension Corporation. These funds will be in individual accounts held by each saver in any one of a number of private schemes or, hopefully, in one of the burgeoning number of mutual-aid organisations. The main function of the pensions corporation is to oversee the universalisation policy. (See **Functions of the Stakeholders' Pension Corporation** below.) Of course a government could attempt to attack these individually-held savings accounts. But to do so would involve a wholly different order of state intervention than that needed to adjust entitlements to unfunded state benefits. Such an intervention would almost certainly be illegal under the European Convention on Human Rights, and in any case impossible to accomplish, given the transfer of private funds involved, without a massive public furore, and an almost certain rout at the following election.

Public opinion has not yet been tested on the question of extending compulsory retirement savings schemes. The question has been asked on long-term care. Overwhelmingly the majority of the public is in favour of pooling risks by establishing a national fund. Similar results, I believe, would be registered for extending funded pension coverage.

Pension Reform Three

Within this compulsory savings framework individuals will be completely free to choose between private-sector companies, a National Savings Scheme and mutually-aided schemes as the vehicles through which they make their long-term savings commitments.

Pension Reform Four

SERPS will be wound up for new accruals at the millennium. In effect the opted-out rebate of 4.6 per cent will be universalised for people earning over £100 and paid into each

contributor's new pensions savings account. Over time those workers not making adequate savings and earning over £100 will be required progressively to raise their savings ratio towards the 16 per cent of income level.

Extending compulsion

How might such a policy of compulsion be achieved? **Making Welfare Work** proposed establishing a Stakeholders' Pension Corporation to spearhead the policy of universalism. An effective policy would see the current element of compulsion extended in four directions. Practically every worker could be brought within the new National Insurance scheme. The saving schemes have to be made universal. But such a policy must be phased in gradually. The level of contributions, similarly staged over time, has to be raised to an adequate level. Another process staged over time would be the fulfilment of a commitment to bring into pension saving schemes those who are currently outside the labour market.

A policy of compulsory savings should be seen for what it is, namely a move to complete the patchwork-like quilt of existing pension provision so that there is a universal coverage in second pensions, and that a growing proportion of second pension coverage should be of a funded nature. Compulsion would be seen not as an innovation, but merely as an extension of existing policy.

The move to include every worker within the National Insurance scheme will itself have a number of important consequences. It will guarantee in future that practically all workers will have in place the first building block of an adequate pension. For the lowest paid, ie those up to £100 a week in current terms, it will be their only pension entitlement unless they make voluntary payments towards a second pension. For those who are on low pay for the whole of their working lives the state pension will provide a high replacement ratio to earnings, ie, on current money terms a pension of £61.15 a week for those earning up to £100 a week. The National Insurance system will therefore be the main agent of redistribution in pension provision. It will do so clearly and has a quite different function from that of ensuring that higher-paid workers themselves save more now for a more adequate pension in the future. For higher-paid workers the state pension will be only part of their retirement income. But for a very large number of workers it will be a substantial part of their retirement income. So while the state retirement pension is of greatest value to those on the lowest income, it will also become an important building block in achieving adequate income in retirement for practically all pensioners. The state pension thereby gains powerful electoral protection.

Individuals have a wide range of levels of economic activity and earnings throughout their lives and also have very different experiences in building up pension entitlement during that period. The Government Actuary has not therefore attempted to produce detailed estimates of how the proposed scheme would affect employees at different income levels. Table 9 below shows the global sums involved, with additional pension savings of £1bn in the year 2000, rising to £6bn in 2020 as the compulsory savings ratio rises by one per cent each year from the 4.6 per cent set at the millennium.

Table 9: Additional pension savings resulting from extending compulsory savings to all workers

Year	£bn
2000	1
2005	3
2010	5
2015	6
2020	6

Source: The Government Actuary's Department

These changes, particularly in the impact of the income base on which the National Insurance contributions are levied, will have an important impact on the workings of the labour market. Currently no contributions are paid by the employer or worker on incomes below the lower earnings level. Not surprisingly, the hike in the tax system at this point affects the number of jobs paying below the insurance threshold. Big companies, like Tesco, are concerned with running their businesses effectively and are as unconcerned about the threshold level as small and newly-established firms are interested in it.

The abolition of the current lower earnings level threshold of £61 and the bringing into the scheme of all weekly earnings above £10 a week are not primarily aimed at raising revenue. These moves will, however, help to meet the relatively small additional cost of awarding pensions to those who would not otherwise gain a pension in their own right and who would not have gained a pension through home responsibility payments or through their husband's contribution. The current system produces the worst of both worlds. A large number of workers gains no insurance coverage in their own right. The tax side offers a considerable incentive to split jobs up into small portions in order to avoid paying the National Insurance levy.

This pension reform will therefore create a level playing field in respect of new job opportunities. Henceforth there will be no incentive to employers to divide up what are currently full-time jobs into packages of part-time work in order to avoid paying National Insurance contributions. Similarly there will be no incentive for new jobs to be tailored in order to gain this tax advantage.

The abolition of SERPS

We have already seen how SERPS has twice suffered the most severe mauling at the hands of the Government, resulting first in the halving of benefit entitlement only for the cost of SERPS again to be cut substantially. Who can say that a future government will not act similarly in further reducing the value of SERPS?

The proposal is that those workers currently in SERPS should, from the millennium onwards, pay what are now their SERPS contributions into a funded pension scheme of their choice. It is at this point that critics of change point to what is called the double-payment issue - namely, the payment to cover both the cost of past SERPS entitlement together with the building-up of individual funded schemes. The costs of meeting such entitlement built up at the closure of the scheme are given in the table below.

Table 10: The costs of future SERPS entitlement with the scheme (a) unreformed and (b) closed in 2000
(£ billion)

Year	Unreformed	Closed
2000	4.2	4.2
2010	8.5	7.5
2020	11.0	9.0
2030	12.0	9.0
2040	10.0	6.5
2050	10.0	3.0

Source: The Government Actuary's Department

Pension Reform Five

Bonds will be issued to cover the extra transition cost over the level of expenditure in 2000 of meeting the accrued SERPS entitlement. These bonds will become payable as the projected SERPS budget falls when a growing number of workers draw pensions from funded pension schemes.

But most of the critics alleging that this strategy involves a double payment exaggerate the point at dispute. Just as there is already widespread compulsion in the current arrangements to ensure adequate second-pension provision, so too do the criticisms of the double costs ignore the extent to which this dual cost is already being paid without any protest whatsoever. Those workers in occupational and private pension schemes are both paying for their own second pension and contributing to the cost of paying out today's National Insurance retirement pension. There is nevertheless an additional cost involved in proposing the closure of SERPS, and this has to be faced. The sooner this is faced the less the consequences will be.

Should these costs be borne entirely by today's and tomorrow's taxpayers? Or should a longer timescale be considered so that we bring into focus the reduction in public expenditure which will result from the closure of SERPS at the millennium? Failure to close SERPS will mean substantial tax bills for future generations. On grounds of equity therefore, the approach adopted here is to move forward the additional costs which will accrue to SERPS from entitlements built up before the scheme is closed at the millennium. It is proposed that long-term Government Bonds be issued each year to cover this additional cost and for these bonds to begin to fall due at a time when tax rates will be appreciably lower than they would otherwise be without the closure of the scheme.

The Contributions Agency will remain as a collection agency and will be of particular value to workers on low earnings. This group will be able to build up capital sums which could then be transferred into the scheme of their choice at, say, twice-yearly intervals thereby minimising collection service costs.

Pension Reform Six

To establish a National Savings Pension Scheme.

Making Welfare Work also proposed that the Pensions Corporation should also establish a National Pensions Savings Scheme, a proposal which was subsequently endorsed by the Social Justice Commission, the Dahrendorf Commission and the Retirement Income Inquiry. Although these organisations changed the name slightly, its functions were essentially the same as attributed to the scheme in **Making Welfare Work.**

Since each of these reports was published a National Savings Pension Scheme Bill has been introduced in Parliament. The aim of the Bill is to establish a simple and safe method for individuals to save for their retirement.[15] The idea is for the Post Office to have the power to sell two kinds of savings agreements. The first would be linked to gilts so that a set rate of return was guaranteed to each block of savings. The second agreement would be for savings to track the FT 'Footsie' Index. In this way savers would have the opportunity to link their pension funds into capital growth at minimum risk. In addition, both forms of savings could be run on very low administrative charges. The scheme will offer savers one of the most competitive price means of building up capital for their retirement and, in this way, hopefully impact favourably on the current general level of charges made on savings within the industry. Pension Reform Six is not that very different from the reform Gladstone attempted over 120 years ago.

Pension Reform Seven

To establish a Stakeholders' Pension Corporation which will have the task of implementing the universalisation of second pension provision for workers earning over £100 a week. The Stakeholders' Pension Corporation will operate alongside a second body established to run as the new National Insurance Corporation. The Pension Corporation's main functions will be fivefold.

Functions of the Stakeholders' Pensions Corporation

The Corporation will have the task of ensuring that the current patchwork of provision - covering occupational pensions as well as personal pensions -

becomes part of this universal coverage. The aim is not to destroy any of the existing funded provisions, but to ensure that they provide adequate pension cover. Adequacy will be measured by the level of contributions paid as a proportion of the person's wage or salary and the length of time over which the contributions will build up, or by a corresponding test for defined benefit schemes.

The second task of the Corporation will be to agree the rate of contributions for employee and employer, as the programme envisages compulsory participation by both parties. Changes in rates will of course need to be given Parliamentary approval to gain the force of law. The contributions would initially be modest, but they would need to be progressively increased. For illustrative purposes the Government Actuary has assumed that contributions will begin at 4.6 per cent of income, and be increased annually by 1 percentage point. The Corporation's board would need to consider this strategy and the extent to which contributions in the initial period should vary according to the age of the contributor.

The ultimate aim is to ensure that around 16 per cent of wages or salaries is set aside into a funded pension scheme, so that an adequate pension awaits everyone at the point of retirement. Part of this adequate pension income will be derived from the National Insurance pension to which everybody earning over the lower earnings level contributes at present. Here is an opportunity to turn the rhetoric of a partnership between the public and private sector into a reality. Abolishing the lower earnings level opens up the opportunity to forge a genuine and lasting link between the state's National Insurance scheme and the universal provision of second pensions.

The proposal to abolish the lower earnings level will result in including all those drawing pay within the state's scheme. This will result in a major subsidy from taxpayers being built into the scheme. It will benefit the very lowest paid and will run alongside the tax subsidy given to all members of funded pension schemes. Every worker will therefore be a member and will be contributing towards the first tier of their pension income. A contributory rate of 2 per cent will be set on the first tranche of earnings.

In addition to both of these functions **Making Welfare Work** proposed that the Pension Corporation would also be responsible for carrying out three additional functions.

- It will be responsible for the SERPS machinery to collect contributions from those employees who wish to have their savings deducted directly from their wage or salary cheque.

- The office of the pension regulator, established by the 1995 Pensions Act, will be transferred to the Corporation. The office will be transformed from the largely passive role envisaged in the Act into a proactive agency determined to root out fraud and malpractice. The Corporation will have a duty to report annually to Parliament on the adequacy of second pension provision as well as on the question of the security of funds.

- The Pensions Corporation will also assume the regulatory role concurrently carried out by the Personal Investment Authority and IMRO. This reform will bring together the existing regulatory role which is dispersed between the two, and, if the Security and Investments Board is included, three organisations. It will be a move towards a long overdue simplification of the regulatory regime. In addition, the Corporation, with the Inland Revenue, will carry out the regulatory role on the new long-term savings account (**Pension Reform Seven**).

Pension Reform Eight

To establish a new savings vehicle which will simplify the operation for the saver while leading also to a simplified tax and regulatory system.

During a recent seminar on simplifying pensions the Prudential[16] suggested creating a new 'safe haven' for pension savings which would:

- attract tax concessions;
- cut regulatory costs because of its simplicity;
- ensure that the competition between providers of a very similar product lead to very substantial reductions in the servicing costs of such savings.

This idea has been developed so that it achieves the objective of simplification, while becoming a major vehicle through which a universalisation of second pensions is achieved. The scheme itself will be a tripartite one with contributions coming from individuals, their employers and from taxpayers who will underwrite the cost of allowing these contributions to be tax-free. It is important to emphasise this tax subsidy which will go to all participants. The twofold subsidy to the poor which is built into the scheme - redistribution through the National Insurance pension and the payment of contributions to second pension schemes of target groups - will not therefore be the only, or indeed the most significant subsidy. Rich and poor alike will be beneficiaries.

From the vesting day of the new scheme, existing tax privileges would cease on all new pensions savings which take place in existing schemes, with one exception which will be explained below. On vesting day all new tax advantages will be limited to a new savings vehicle. This will allow savings to take place up to a limit of £6,000 a year which will attract tax concessions at the standard rate. While voluntary savings above this level will be without tax inducements, the legal and regulatory structure will offer the same protection to these funds as it will for that part of the life savings and pensions account which attracts tax bonuses.

Most of my constitutents to whom I have spoken about their personal pension provisions have no idea about the type of scheme of which they are members. In exasperation they will say 'it is like a building society savings account'. The new lifetime and pensions savings account builds on what I believe most voters understand to be the basis of their personal pensions - a simple savings account. This simplification will have a major pay-off in terms of cost. Together with the competition between existing pension and life insurance companies, and hopefully the advance of a new wave of mutual-aid societies, the charges for servicing these accounts will fall. With compulsion the need to sell pensions ceases in its current form. Savers will be looking for companies, rather than the reverse. Furthermore, this simplification of the mechanics of savings will itself lead to a dramatic simplification in the current structure of regulation. The inspection of lifetime savings based on a simple savings account minimises the chances of the provider breaking the law or any of the regulatory authorities' rules of practice. It also makes it that much easier and quicker to pick up any irregularities.

So, a move which sets out to offer a much simpler and more understandable means of long-term savings also:

- becomes a means of making a start in restructuring financial regulation, pushing down the cost of such regulation while at the same time increasing its effectiveness;

- sets a limit to the tax privileges for long-term savings in a way which does not penalise voluntary savings above this level. The Inland Revenue would cease to be concerned about whether individuals are making contributions to schemes which take their pension income above two-thirds of their final salary. The Revenue's concern will be with the operation and running of the new system of tax bonuses;

- simplifies the policing of schemes. As each person would have an Inland Revenue tax allowance account to draw upon, no-one would unintentionally place themselves beyond the law - as they currently do - by saving in excess of this amount in different pension schemes or, because of their changed employment position - from employed to self-employed or vice versa - be members of an inappropriate savings scheme and thereby wrongly claim tax concessions.

Each person would hold a lifetime savings and pension tax allowance account with the Revenue. Existing schemes of pension provision would draw on these accounts to finance current tax advantages. Existing members of personal pension schemes would similarly draw on their lifetime savings and pension tax allowance account to enhance their current personal pension provision. So too would employers making contributions to their employees' savings accounts.

Any one year's unspent tax allowances will be transferrable and rolled up for other years. Individuals able to draw only part of the value of these allowances in any one year will therefore be able to draw upon them when, perhaps, their income is higher. How these tax allowances might be converted as deposits in the lifetime savings and pensions accounts of the very low-paid as they draw their capital at retirement will be discussed in follow up seminars to **How To Pay For The Future**.

The Inland Revenue function as tax bonus dispenser and regulator suggests how this pivotal role needs very little development for it to become the record keeper of the universalisation of second-pension provision. It would be to the Revenue that the new Pensions Corporation would turn for its record-keeping activities.

Savings, not taxation

It is important that the new life-time savings and pensions account is discussed in a way which informs rather than deceives voters about the new shape of welfare. This initiative is about:

- forging a new partnership between public and private sectors;
- establishing a stakeholders' welfare state where individual benefits are linked more clearly to contributions held in personalised accounts;
- breaking down the inflexibility of today's welfare state, where rights under pay-as-you-go schemes are locked in only to be drawn upon at some distant future point;
- and thereby winning support for compulsory savings (paid into one's own account) to take the place of compulsory taxation (often to pay the people who have not saved).

One key aspect of **Making Welfare Work**'s proposed reforms was that lifetime savings and pensions should be a genuine savings scheme. The savings will be owned by the individual and not by the state. It is impossible to overestimate the importance of this point. Without stakeholder status stemming from ownership, the reform is likely to receive a sour reaction from voters. They will view it as another wheeze to increase taxation. **The stakeholder principle is about ushering in a new welfare era where collective provision is achieved through individualised ownership and effort.**

To signify the dimension of this change from old to new welfare, one duty of the Pensions Corporation will be to debate with the providers of second funded pensions the rights of savers under the new scheme. The lifetime savings and pension scheme must be seen as a savings operation, and the essence of savings is the ability to draw upon them or to use them.

Making Welfare Work proposed that in agreed circumstances contributors should be able to borrow from or use their capital stake in their funded scheme as a guarantee when they wish to borrow. This aspect of the scheme will clearly define compulsory savings as being a very different operation from compulsory taxation, where there will be no pension capital accumulation and therefore no rights to borrow against such sums. While the clear overriding objective of the welfare reconstruction is to ensure that adequate savings for retirement remain in place, there should be clearly defined rights to borrow against this capital over a person's working life.

This right would be additional to the clearly defined circumstances when the whole of the pension capital can be drawn upon before retirement, eg when a person is fatally ill. While the Pension Corporation will be the body to initiate this debate, two areas should be considered for loans. The right to draw against pension capital to secure a deposit on a house purchase is one. Another will be to meet training fees which an individual needs to finance for the development of their career. This borrowing aspect - allowing a compulsory scheme to adapt to individual circumstances - ensures that some of the advantage which stem from a purely voluntary pension savings scheme such as operates in New Zealand are built into the reconstruction of welfare proposed in **Making Welfare Work**.

Pension Reform Nine

The extension of pension savings opens up the possibility of building new mutually-aided, commercially-run organisations owned and directed by the membership themselves. This reform will help recreate a sense of social cohesion in tune with the members' wishes and expectation.

While the new long-term savings vehicle offers the private sector equal access to operate in the new scheme, it also offers the possibility of a renaissance of mutual-aid schemes which will be established to accompany the advent of compulsory savings for retirement incomes. These schemes will be organised on different levels:

- nationally, as some friendly societies are currently constituted;
- industrially, with membership being drawn from workers in that sector, such as catering or building workers;
- geographically, with membership coming from contributors in one area;
- by interest groups, like trade unions, offering membership of their mutual aid schemes as a major fringe benefit.

Friendly societies

Making Welfare Work's aim was for friendly societies and mutual-aid societies to be able to participate fully in the new welfare state.

What might therefore at first sight appear to be a straightforward welfare reform assumes a much wider significance. The reform becomes one which is concerned not only with channels of welfare, but also with organising that welfare in such a way as to impart values of social cohesion and solidarity. Because of probable widespread support for them, existing and new mutual-aid organisations would become not merely agents safely transferring incomes from periods at work to other parts of a person's lifetime, but of doing so in a manner which strengthens rather than weakens Britain's sense of social cohesion. It is worth remembering that friendly-society membership is presently larger than the number of people who pay trade union dues.

Friendly societies and mutual aid funds are:

- membership-run. They thereby advance the stakeholder principle of greater control over the financial aspects of our lives

- potentially low-cost organisations. This derives in part from members undertaking some of the running of the organisation themselves. Friendly societies and mutual aid bodies can be low-cost organisations because there are no shareholders to pay. Profits are ploughed back into new or higher benefits.

- commercially-orientated. Commercial considerations are a crucial part of mutual aid and friendly society operations. But with friendly societies the profits go to the membership rather than the shareholders.

- agents of social cohesion. By their very nature friendly societies are membership societies or they are nothing. They are inclusive bodies, thriving on participation, cooperation and partnership. These are values which need promotion and are a crucial part of welfare's reconstruction.

- genuine risk-sharing organisations. Friendly societies spread risks between members in a way which private insurance organisations do not.

So, for example, police officers in Northern Ireland facing greater risk than those on the mainland of being killed during 'the troubles' were not charged higher insurance premiums by their friendly society, as they would have been by any ordinary insurance company.

- channels of service. Friendly societies are a major source of voluntary help. The fundamental importance of this fact in an age of growing frailty for most of us towards the end of our long lives, and the potential it offers for combining voluntary effort with meeting a growing public need, will be highlighted in the follow-up volume.

Making compulsion work

In Britain a successful universalisation of second pensions needs to be organised around a four-part strategy. No one part is omnipotent, and no one part is without importance. Each is mutually supportive. The different parts consist of:

- use of the law
- role of education
- part played by incentives
- triggers towards universalism

The first part of this strategy is to use the law. On vesting day all workers will become members contributing to the basic state retirement scheme. In addition, the Pensions Corporation will have a duty of overseeing the universalisation of second-pension provision. It will have the duty of setting the contribution rates for the employer and employee for those workers not currently within a company or personal scheme and who are earning above £100 per week. It will also set the employer rate for contributions to personal pension schemes where they are currently not paid. The issue of how contributions will be divided between employer and employee will be a major subject in the follow-up volume to **How To Pay For The Future**.

The introduction and discussion of the Bill making contributions to second pensions compulsory will also serve as part of a wide-scale education campaign on this key change in policy. A draft Pension (Universalisation) Bill could be published early in the new Parliament. The Pensions Bill should not proceed to a Second Reading until after it has been to the Social Security Select Committee

further proposal is made for a clear Exchequer subsidy to pay for long-term sick and disabled to have their pension fund contributions paid as well.

The initial cost of making a second pension provision for carers depends on the numbers who will be claiming invalid care allowance. Evidence from the recent past shows how easy it is for individuals to move between the categories of unemployed and long-term sick and/or disabled in an attempt to maximise their income. Similar movement could be expected with the introduction of the payment of pension contributions for identified groups outside the labour market. The gatekeeping role in controlling eligibility for the invalid care allowance, and to the new care pension, will therefore be very important in maintaining the budgetary costs of this reform.

Given these uncertainties, it is advisable to quote potential costs on illustrative assumptions for the numbers for whom such pension costs might be payable. It is assumed that the numbers qualifying for ICA would increase significantly from the current total of about 400,000. For both this group, and the wider group into which it will evolve when the care pension proposals take effect, the pension contributions are based on a £150 a week wage. (See later for care pension proposals.)

The cost of making contributions for the first group of carers from year one of the scheme (2000) to 2050 are given in the table below.

Table 11: Extra pension contributions in respect of carers *(£ million)*

Year	£m
2000	50
2010	150
2020	170
2030	170
2040	170
2050	170

Source: The Government Actuary's Department.

A programme for the left

Serious consideration of the mutual-aid option is not an attempt to conjure up nostalgia amongst the electorate. It is to combine the best social traditions of the past 100 years or more. **Making Welfare Work** aims to marry Attlee's inclusiveness and comprehensiveness with those attributes of individual responsibility and initiative which were the hallmarks of the pre-Attlee settlement, and which are themselves once again registering strongly with voters' preferences.

In addition, the policy aims at strengthening Burke's little platoons. This pension reform will bring into existence a large number of new organisations, many of which will be friendly society and mutual aid bodies. Here will also be a major opportunity for unions to refashion still further their range of functions and to reach parts of the workforce unused to contact with them.

To say therefore that this reform offers trade unions a new role is perhaps to approach the issue from the wrong end. Friendly Societies were a precursor of, and their functions became a mainstay of, the trade union movement. Increasingly, however, trade unions were stripped of their welfare role as their activities were increasingly taken over by the state. At a time when the unions are radically rethinking what their role might be in an economy where overwhelmingly new jobs are being formed in the medium-sized or small firm sector, thereby making the traditional stance of collective bargaining difficult if not impossible to advance, the proposals in **Making Welfare Work** offer a new agenda. A membership-service approach, which would involve the reinventing of the friendly society role for trade unions, rather than a simple wage bargaining line, will hopefully be part of their thinking.

This option offers as many attractions to society at large as it does to the unions. A rebuilding of non-state services is urgent. Despite their recent decline, trade unions still have a total membership of around 8 million. If the unions are to prevent a further erosion of their base they badly need a revised and expanded approach to their purpose and functions. Civil society also needs the existence of well-functioning bodies able to provide services which are independent of the state. Political society needs the re-inventing of civil associations if a more decentralised political culture is again to take root.

So the pension debate enters into the wider discussion about how best to rebuild Britain's political institutions. A major pension reform which, at the very least, has a mutual aid component, offers voters the very sense of control over their own affairs for which an increasing number are looking. It is also an approach which by its very nature strengthens an acceptance of a responsibility to other members of society. It engenders a sense of personal improvement. Moreover, it is an approach which encourages individual advance and autonomy in a manner that fosters a community-based ethic.

Left-wing critics of the approach advocated here are still captured by the old statist approach where quick, wide-ranging reforms governed from the centre are sacrosanct. The urgency and the need for the most radical, wide-ranging changes are not in dispute. What is at stake is how best such changes can be brought about and then sustained. Is it going to be once again a top-down, imposed reform, or one built up on a bottom-up approach, where more and more individuals become the main driving force of reform and thereby enhance the chances of success?

Making Welfare Work argued that there are, sadly, no short cuts or easy fixes. If welfare is to be reconstructed the changes must:

- Go with the grain of human nature rather than attempt to deny the most powerful of inherent motivational forces.

- Accept that the state has become increasingly less able to command and implement grand strategies for change.

- Recognise that what was above all wrong with post-war welfare settlement was the exclusion of individual responsibility and initiative.

- Positively foster self-improvement, which is a crucial component of any country attempting to rebuild itself.

The universalisation of second-pension provision as advocated in **Making Welfare Work** has relevance also to the new industry strategy which Labour's treasury team is designing. The Australian scheme for partial compulsion has already resulted in an increase in the savings ratio in that country. The availability of a larger supply of long-term savings does not by itself guarantee future higher levels of investment in areas which pay handsome dividends. But it opens up that possibility, which would be absent without compulsion. Reforming welfare is not therefore a one-off, compartmentalised reform. It should rather be seen as a crucial reform:

- in its own right in respect of redefining our concept of welfare;
- in defining the relationship between the individual and the state, and thereby the nature of both civil and political society;
- as one which relates to the other main objective to which Labour is committed, namely rebuilding Britain's much depleted economic strength.

2. Stakeholders' Insurance Scheme

Making Welfare Work proposed that a new system of insurance benefits should be initiated and administered by a Stakeholders' Insurance Corporation. The objective is for this body to be clearly independent of government. A follow-up volume will look in more detail at the constitution of the new mutually owned Insurance Corporation.

How can a safe transition be carried out from today's system to tomorrow's promise? Here an outline is given where the building of a new system should commence, what organisational framework is necessary for its success and how the emerging new scheme could initially run in tandem with existing National Insurance provisions. Each of these three issues is considered in turn.

The aim of each reform in **Making Welfare Work** was to have maximum impact in breaking means-tested dependency and minimising the attack on decent values which means tests generate. With this in mind, it is proposed that the new Insurance Corporation should in the first instance be responsible for two new benefits - a care pension and an unemployment insurance scheme.

While both benefits have a joint role in restructuring welfare, they also have individual roles in achieving this objective. The new care pension is aimed at meeting a new need stemming from a growth in the numbers of very frail elderly matched only by the Government's decision generally to limit patient care to a short-term only basis within NHS hospitals. The NHS long-term care function has been directed to the largely private residential and nursing home sector. Here patients are charged for their care and the reform aims to break the dominance of means-testing in this area.

The new Unemployment Insurance aims to counter the pressures a rapidly-changing job market has recently placed on large numbers of workers. Here the objective is to structure welfare so that an individual's self-interest simultaneously promotes the public good ie to cease being unemployed at the first opportunity. The risk-taking of getting back into work in today's labour market is supported by a new insurance scheme granting a fast track re-insurance cover to those attempting to regain a foothold back in the labour market.

Care Pension Insurance

Care Pension Reform One

To extend pension coverage to all ICA recipients.

Care Pension Reform Two

To introduce a non-means-tested care pension for those requiring residential or nursing care.

Practically everybody will draw a pension. Only a small minority of us will require paid intensive care at the end of our lives. This fundamental difference in our needs should be reflected in the Welfare State. While everybody needs to save for their retirement, it is absurd to insist that savings also take place to cover the cost of long-term care which five out of six individuals on current estimates will not need. Here in fact is an emerging need which can most effectively and cheaply be delivered by way of a new national benefit, although one which is again kept outside the declining State welfare system.

A correspondent outlines the case for a care pension. Like so many letters which have been written since **Making Welfare Work**'s publication, it emphasises how the existing system of means-tests is schooling citizens in all the wrong lessons. This correspondent, writing from Altrincham, contrasts the behaviour and treatment of two sets of relatives. The first was of:

> *an elderly relative, childless and widowed. While married the couple [had] lived a prudent and careful life throughout, paying all state dues and taxes as demanded. They took out a mortgage in the early to mid 1930s and owned fully their own home until they retired, when my parents helped them with funding to move closer to younger members of*

the family for ultimate support in the future. Over a decade ago we moved this then isolated and widowed relative to be closer for support from us. Four years ago this person could not cope in spite of our close support and wished strongly to live in a nursing home, but out of this area and, for some inexplicable reason, closer to her initial retirement town where the fees are lower than in this area.

We were unable to get any state help, such as meals on wheels, home help, nor a district nurse on a regular basis to ease the burden whilst the relative lived close to us. When we wished to go away on holiday we had to pay from our own resources for the aged relative to have cover and ultimately to go into a nursing home. Our GP seemed unable to assist materially in these problems. So much for the welfare state.

At the last house move, and by agreement with the relative, we safeguarded the significant sums of our family money invested in the house in which the relative lived. Otherwise I presume the greedy state would have attempted to gobble up our trapped capital and we might have been unable easily, if at all, to convince the authorities of the true situation and thus release our own money.

The nursing home fees are at present in excess of £1200 per month which regrettably the state does not fund fully. Accordingly, we are faced with making up the shortfall which amounts usually to about £200 a month. My wife, my brother and I feel the state has and is continuing to fail totally to honour its welfare obligations to this aged relative (and by inference to ourselves for we are not the aged relative's descendants). This relative now has the minimum amount of a fluctuating £3000 in a current account which we manage.

The second contrasting case is of another relative, this time an aunt and uncle. The uncle was called up during the 1939-45 war and served honourably in the forces abroad. When demobilised into a 'land fit for heroes to live in' they decided that as they had served the state obediently as demanded of them, they would not save, but having survived the war, like many of their generation, they would enjoy life to the full as far as their taxed income would allow. Their attitude, frequently expressed in my presence, has been that 'we have done our bit for the state, paid our taxes and our dues, and the rest is up to the state to provide for us!' With the immediate post-war pronouncements about state welfare who could blame them?

This couple have spent every penny of their taxed income, had foreign holidays years ago when many of their type did not go abroad, have lived since demobilisation in subsidised council housing, and now dwell in local authority sheltered accommodation. I doubt whether they will have any assets whatsoever to leave their children, and suspect that the state may even have to bury them.

While previously ... I have deprecated such an attitude to profligacy now I can sympathise with their behaviour, especially when comparing the treatment they have had and are getting with that meted out to the other older relative.

In the light of these experiences should we abandon our aged relative and see what happens, for that relative is in reality not my responsibility. It is only our continuing response to my late mother's wishes that we should care for this relative that has put us in this position. What would happen if we failed to make the supplementary payment? Would the person in question be thrown out into the streets? What would the state do as a response? Should we spend/dissipate our own hard-earned taxed funds in a series say, of round the world trips, comparing the trips by Concorde with that by the QEII, rather than saving it for the future, as so to enjoy the results of our taxed labour rather than allow the state effectively to confiscate it later?

The state at present seems not to encourage prudence and investment by its confiscatory behaviour which, surely, in the long run, must be wrong. The present situation makes life even more of a lottery. If you die young then fortunately your children can at least inherit something. If you are unlucky enough to survive to become geriatric then you are likely to have nothing left to will to one's offspring. This seems to be an argument for euthanasia.

Again the message is pretty stark. What lessons, this correspondent asks rhetorically, should he draw from the behaviour of these two sets of relatives?

Should he and his wife continue to be moral citizens, to cut down on luxury holidays, continue buying their own home and save all they can? Or is it better to assume the taxpayers are a soft touch, spend all they can and let welfare pick up the bill?

The answer in **Making Welfare Work** was unequivocal. It is as necessary now as ever to have a welfare system which supports work, initiative, effort, savings and honesty. There is a further criterion by which the new welfare should be judged. Are we aiming to create a welfare state which also values inheritance? Or is it right and wise to think more seriously in individualistic terms only; that a person will expect to exhaust their income and savings during their own lifetime? Or is inheritance one of those unappreciated webs which binds families and friends together thereby knitting individuals into society both horizontally, ie to people living now, and vertically, gaining from the past and handing on capital into the future?

Making Welfare Work was again unequivocal. Except for the very foolish or bitter, the rich have always been able to pass on capital from generation to generation. Now, with rising national income, and a genuine property-owning democracy, inheritance, albeit on a much more modest scale, is within the grasp of a clear majority of the population. **Making Welfare Work** believed that the opportunity for a very significant group of the population to build up a capital base should not be lost through penal welfare confiscatory rules. Nor did **Making Welfare Work** see the creation of a class of grandparents who misreport their assets in order that they evade welfare's confiscatory rules as anything but an undesirable outcome. **Making Welfare Work**'s welfare model for the millennium is one where income is gained from work, capital and welfare - in that order.

In proposing a reconstitution of welfare in **Making Welfare Work**, a new care pension and unemployment insurance were chosen to initiate the new insurance scheme. Here the maximum impact could be made in respect of unemployment insurance by preventing an entire household being without work. A new unemployment insurance would link previous efforts at work to benefit. It would also prevent other members of the household from feeling it necessary to work and lie about their earnings, as the incentives in a means-tested scheme presently teach claimants.

Similarly the introduction of a care pension would change people's expectations. Under the present system of a means-tested community care programme, all of the incentives deter claimants from saving, or of being honest about the value of their assets.

It is true that, in contrast to many of our partners in Europe, the impact of a severe ageing of the population's profile is already well advanced. It is nevertheless expected to continue apace in the coming decade. While ageing is not the only factor influencing the demand for nursing and residential care (fast becoming one of the most costly items in the welfare budget), it is by far the most dominant. It has already led the Government to make what is likely to be the most significant alteration to the NHS since its inception in 1948.

An assumption on which the Service was founded was that most of the care being offered would be short-term. It inherited the geriatric beds when the NHS was formed in 1948. But for decades this hospital population was fairly static. As the number of geriatric patients rose, however, the Government deflected the pressure on NHS budgets by allowing poorer pensioners additional supplementary benefit payments to cover the cost of residential care.

As that bill exploded the Government, in typical fashion, panicked, transferring the task of deciding who would qualify for assistance to local authorities. It cash-limited the budget after generously increasing it. Now the Government has issued guidelines laying down that the charges should be met where possible from beneficiaries. A free service has been transformed, almost without debate, into a means-tested one.

A number of options are being actively considered so that care costs can be covered. These are:

• Continuing to cover the cost by way of means-tested benefit;

• Encouraging private insurance to cover this risk;

• Adapting private and company pension provision so that payments are weighted to the end of a pensioner's life;

- Allowing pensioners to realise their housing capital to meet the costs of long-term care;

- Introducing a new National Insurance benefit through the new stakeholders insurance scheme which is non-means-tested.

Making Welfare Work argued against adopting all but one of these options. The present provision of means-tested assistance towards care costs is having a predictable outcome: all the pressures are on families to transfer assets before they are gobbled up in care costs.

If this policy of avoidance could be universalised there might be something to be said in favour of it. But some elderly pensioners and their families still believe that fiddling or working the system is wrong. That does not mean, however, that there is no resentment to the penal tax rates on their truthfulness. Far from it.

Then again, the rules against deliberately divesting oneself of capital in order to qualify for means-tested help are not universally applied. I have met senior social workers whose policy it is when families apply for help for an elderly relative to recommend a friendly solicitor in order to transfer the family's capital. This statement is no misprint. In many areas capital is still regarded as being held by a family rather than it being placed in individual ownership, and this is most clearly seen in farming and crofting communities. Indeed, the loss of capital in these circumstances would lead to large numbers of the extended family being made unemployed. Hence the advice by the local authority official whose duty in fact is to collect as much money as possible for fees for nursing and/or residential care.

The unfairness of the present means-tested system is part of the case against continuing the current approach. There is also a more positive argument. **Making Welfare Work** saw the building-up of capital ownership amongst a wider group of the population as a sign of a successfully strong and vibrant society. Far from viewing life as something entirely self-sufficient, and where each generation is expected to produce and consume its entire produce, **Making Welfare Work** saw the strong links between familial generations as fundamental to any group which wishes and is able to consider itself a society. Means tests, applying as they do against income and capital, strike at the very heart of this concept of a good society.

Making Welfare Work did not argue against the second option - ie private insurance - on dogmatic grounds. The practical case against this approach is what counts. While there is a growing discussion and interest amongst some insurance companies about the kind of product which might be provided, there is still little interest amongst consumers. In part this is because it is very difficult to persuade young people to put aside income now towards a care pension which will not be drawn for another 40 years, if then. It is also because many of the policies so far on offer still see the state as playing a fall-back role after the care pension has been drawn for a period of usually three years. None of the policies which are on offer at reasonable cost provides what is most desired from such a contract: the certainty that the policy will be adequate in covering care costs for as long as that care is needed. I cannot therefore see the private sector making much inroad in this area despite the recently announced Government initiative.[17] Moreover, the private sector is likely in the near future to have its work more than cut out in offering savings vehicles for the universal second pension proposals which **Making Welfare Work** put forward.

A similar line of reasoning suggests there is likely to be little headway made with the idea that second pensions should be weighted towards the end rather than the start of a period of retirement. No matter how sensible such a change would be, the question is whether it is realistic to propose such a change. Talking of reforming pensions along these lines underestimates the size of the challenge we still have to face in providing adequate universal second pensions. The central issue is whether current incomes are high enough to ensure a savings rate which will give rise to an adequate universal second pension. Providing a high enough retirement income which can be weighted for set years late in retirement is simply not an option for the vast majority of the population.

At the moment, of course, the very opposite of what should happen to the flow of pension income occurs. The offer of a tax-free lump sum of pension capital to be withdrawn at the start of retirement means that a person's capital is not only reduced by up to a fifth, but it also divorces income flow from need. The case for withdrawing, over time, this major tax concession is made both on grounds of consistency (tax-free contributions should result in taxed benefits, not in a range of taxed and tax-free benefits) and also on grounds of discouraging a major depletion of pension capital at a time of relative affluence for most pensioners. The right to withdraw a portion of pension capital as a lump sum should be retained, but the tax-free status should be progressively withdrawn over a ten-year period.

Similarly, while it is sensible to experiment with ways in which those pensioners who wish to eat into their housing capital can do so, this approach is unlikely to play a major part in underwriting the cost of long-term care. Quite simply, the majority of pensioners do not think that their capital should be used in this manner. Succeeding generations of pensioners will feel the same, whatever the polls may show about their current beliefs and preferences for groups for whom retirement may be up to four decades away. The discussion therefore comes full circle back to a consideration of introducing a new insurance benefit to cover the cost of long-term care. What form might it take?

- **A German model?**

The National Insurance system in Britain owes a great deal (although not everything) to the original development of the concept in Germany. In this case it would again be useful to look east for ideas. Despite the major economic costs associated with reunification, the German Parliament introduced, in January 1995, a new long-term care insurance scheme.

For a decade prior to the reform there had been a debate in Germany about the needs of a growing group of elderly pensioners who were often living alone, but who also needed assistance if their independence was to be safeguarded. This group was growing both relatively and absolutely, while the proportion of three generations living together in one household was becoming less common. In addition, the almost doubling of the 75/85-year-old cohort in a decade, and the increasing ability of medical technology to keep people alive, even if the quality of that life was impaired, imposed an enormous financial burden on local authorities who were the agents reponsible for care. Prior to the reform up to a third of their budgets were being swallowed up in funding care costs.

The lack of a care pension was having an impact on hospital beds too. Estimates vary, but anywhere from between 40,000 to 60,000 elderly people were kept in hospital beds simply because there was no or very inadequate care for them in their own homes. It was feared that this blocking of beds would grow and affect more generally German health services.

Why did Germany adopt an insurance-funded approach? The answer is that it did so for almost the same reason that it adopted the insurance model in the first place, under Bismarck. The German Chancellor then had no direct taxing powers; hence Bismarck's offer of a new deal via an insurance scheme.

This time the Federal Government could have followed the tax route in order to finance new benefits. But, after reunification and the increased tax bills which followed in its wake, the tax model was rejected largely for two reasons. First, adding to direct taxes would have been exceedingly unpopular. Second, there was a worry that a tax backlash following the implementation of new taxes to finance the benefit could result in a totally inadequate pension being paid in the first place, or demands for cuts in the benefits soon afterwards.

The German reform was phased in in two stages. Funding of the new benefit began in January 1995 and the first stage of a two-stage programme was introduced four months later. The payment of the home care benefit began on 1 April 1995 and the institutional care benefit came into operation on 1 July 1996.

The German system makes a crucial distinction - which the British reform would be wise to follow - between the need for what they call basic care, for which people may qualify for help from the new benefit scheme, on the one hand, and medical and treatment care - and later with the introduction of the second stage, the rent and living costs - on the other.

The need for basic care provision is established in one or more respects:

- bodily care, for example regarding help with regard to washing and bathing;
- nutritional care, where claimants need assistance in preparing and eating a suitable diet;
- mobility, where help in getting up, dressing, undressing, walking and climbing stairs are all covered;
- domestic care, concerned with actions such as shopping, cleaning,

washing dishes.

In assessing eligibility three thresholds are considered:

Category 1. Persons in considerable need of long-term care have to establish their need for assistance once a day for at least two activities in the areas of bodily care, nutrition, mobility, together with the need for several activities each week for domestic care.

Category 2. Persons in severe need of long-term care have to establish their need for assistance three times a day at different times for bodily care, nutrition or mobility, together with the additional need for assistance in domestic care.

Category 3. Persons in extreme need of long-term care have to establish their need for round-the-clock care, together with assistance in domestic care.

In order properly to define the three categories of care the following time requirements must also be fulfilled by the person providing the help.

Category 1. At least one and a half hours a day which includes at least 45 minutes' basic care.
Category 2. At least three hours a day of care.
Category 3. At least five hours a day of care.

Given the British experience of an overall steadily improving national record on morbidity, paralleled by a sharply rising rate of successful applications for disability benefits, the gatekeeping functions to eligibility for any benefit, particularly a new one, are of considerable importance. In the German system the medical decisions made to establish eligibility for benefit are carried out by doctors, nursing staff, social workers and psychologists employed by the social fund. Other evidence submitted in support of an application is considered, for example from the applicant's doctor. But the final decision on eligibility rests with the fund, and the fund's staff normally make an examination of the applicant in his or her home before arriving at a decision.

- **Home Care Benefit**

Home Care Benefit comes in three forms. First, there is a monetary benefit which is paid at three rates:

DM400 a month for persons in considerable need of long-term care;
DM800 a month for persons in severe need of long-term care;
DM1300 a month for persons in extreme need of long-term care.

The cash payment is made directly to the successful claimant who can spend the care pension as they wish. It is up to the claimant to pass the benefit on to those providing the care as a reward or as a wage. The allowance is not taxable.

Alternatively the applicant may seek to be awarded a benefit in kind valued again according to need. There are three rates:
up to DM750 a month for persons in considerable need of long-term care (Category 1);
up to DM1800 a month for persons in severe need of long-term care (Category 2);
up to DM2800 a month for persons in extreme need of long-term care with additions up to DM3750 a month in cases of particular hardship (Category 3).
The cost of the package of care is paid for by the insurance fund up to the value of the award. Costs above that award have to be met by the claimant.

As a third possibility, a claimant may go for a 'mixed bag' of part cash and part care. A person in need of extreme long-term care (Category 3) would receive, for example, 60 care visits valued at DM1860 (that is two-thirds of the possible benefit in kind) plus one third of the nursing allowance valued at DM433.

Once the choice of benefit is made, cash, or care, or a combination of both, that person stays on that provision for six months, after which the claimant once again undergoes a medical to decide eligibility and the level of need. At this point a successful claimant is entitled to change the form in which the care is taken.

Successful claimants also gain access to other benefits:

DM2800 is provided once a year to cover the cost of a substitute carer when the carer takes his or her holiday.

The carer's pension contribution, ranging from DM200 to DM600 a month, is covered from the insurance fund. The amount depends on the category into which the claimant is assessed. The care provided has to be in the order of at least 14 hours a week. In addition, this care work is covered by an accident insurance scheme.

In addition the long-term care insurance fund also assumes the cost of nursing aids, such as wheelchairs, special care beds and lifting devices, together with help from any care-related conversion of the home up to a cost of DM5000 for each conversion which is approved.

From July 1996 the second stage of the reform came into play. Benefits of up to DM2800 a month are provided for institutional care. In exceptional cases, and in order to avoid hardship, up to DM3300 a month will be provided if a person is in extreme need of long-term care. Again it is important to stress that the benefit for those needing residential care covers only the cost of the care. The rent and living costs will have to be borne by the person who qualifies for this benefit.

- **No financial crisis**

Despite views widely circulating in this country, the information I gained when visiting Germany in December 1995 was that the fund is not running into immediate financial difficulties. There are a number of reasons for this. The scheme is in its infancy; it only opened for business in April 1995. The Government did not undertake the costings of the scheme - there is no equivalent of the Government Actuary in Germany - and the social partners in making their calculations erred on the side of caution.

While all these reasons play some part in accounting for the surplus in the German scheme, a further cause is probably the most important in explaining the scheme's financial solvency. As we have seen, the scheme allows for a lower rate of cash, with claimants buying precisely the range and form of care they need, or a higher-value benefit which is paid in services. 83 per cent of claimants - far beyond the proportion actually budgeted for - have opted for the lower cash benefit.

Here is an important lesson when planning a new care pension for Britain. The Independent Living Fund was introduced in Britain in 1988. Its funding was later substantially increased only to be abolished, ironically, as part of the Government's community care proposals - for the Fund was providing community care long before the Government hit on that particular buzz phrase.

The payments were often modest, but covered crucial needs of claimants and their families. For a family, for example, where a mother was being night-nursed by a rota of children, payments from the fund were made to cover the cost of neighbours undertaking this task at weekends. The respite care thereby gained for the team of daughters was enough to ensure that this form of care survived until the mother died.

If the cash allowances are paid at a high enough level, but below what the provision of services would cost, another possibility opens up. The option arises that one member of the family may wish to surrender their job in order to become the full time carer. Given the number of people in low-paid jobs, this may mean in many instances that the family income does not fall, and indeed, in some cases, it would rise. Moreover, as the proposal in **Making Welfare Work** was for defined groups of carers to have their pension contributions met, the package could be attractive for the carer, would strengthen families, and would cost less than institutional care.

Care Pension Reform One

Carers claiming ICA will have a pension contribution paid on the notional earnings of £150 a week.

Stage one of the reform is to pay the pension entitlements to those carers claiming the Invalid Care Allowance. In costing this reform the current level of beneficiaries, of around 400,000, has been taken. It is assumed that pension contributions will be paid on a salary of £150 a week. The cost of this reform is put by the Government Actuary at £50m at the millennium, rising to £150m by 2010 and £170m a year by 2020.

Care Pension Reform Two

To introduce a non-means-tested care pension for those requiring residential or nursing care.

The care pension reform needs to be taken in two stages. The most pressing need is to disengage from the current means-tested provision for all the reasons which have been given above. The costings by the Government Actuary of introducing a care pension to replace the present community care provisions run by local authorities is as follows.

The Government Actuary has assumed that the conditions attaching to entitlement to Care Pensions would, at this initial stage at least, result in the numbers entitled including virtually all those currently in long-term care places. It is clear that the proposals would involve a radical change in the potential provision of care in the United Kingdom and recent experience has shown that the market is very sensitive to such changes. The assumption of the numbers entitled is therefore highly uncertain and so this working assumption should only be taken to give a potential outcome if the conditions of entitlement were set at the appropriate level.

There are likely to be some people currently in long-term care places who would fail the eligibility requirements and some who are currently in their own homes who would be eligible. As quoted in the recent House of Commons Health Select Committee report on long-term care, there were in 1994 465,000 long-term care places in the NHS, residential and nursing homes, of which 37,500 were NHS places. The total cost of the non-NHS places, based on average annual costs of nursing homes and residential homes in England as estimated by Laing and Buisson is some £6.2 billion. If those currently in NHS places were to be eligible at the average rate of those currently in nursing care, the cost would rise to about £7 billion, although there would be a corresponding reduction in NHS costs.

It is reasonable to assume that some people who currently remain at home but who require substantial care and would satisfy the future eligibility tests would take up the option of residential or care places (assuming such places were available).

Although it is proposed to consider how the Care Pensions might be extended to people remaining in their own homes in the follow-up to this volume, until such an option is available it is necessary to assume that some allowance must be made for higher care place demand at this stage. Clearly this is critically dependent upon the eligibility rules, but it is not unreasonable to assume that the costs of residential care might be increased by some 25 per cent, and that the total costs in current terms would be of the order of £8 billion. This cost could be covered by a 3 per cent charge on the insurance base and the reduction in care costs financed by taxpayers at present could be matched by a cut in direct taxation.

In the planned follow-up study to **How To Pay For The Future,** the next stage of this reform will be considered. This will allow people needing extensive care to remain for a longer time in their own homes should they wish to do so. The study will also consider how effective gatekeepers can be established in order to control the rise in the budget for stage one of the reform and for this second-stage proposal.

Unemployment insurance

The aim of unemployment insurance reform is twofold. The new scheme must take account of the changing job markets where large numbers of people move quite frequently between jobs. How can these workers have their living standards protected during periods between jobs? The reform must also attempt to cut off the supply route to long-term household dependency, whereby once unemployment insurance cover is lost the household often gains a greater income from means-tested benefits if the partner of the unemployed person also ceases to work.

Unemployment insurance reform

The aim is to provide six-month insurance cover with new qualifying conditions which reward claimants taking risks in getting back into work.

- **The record**

What has been the pattern of unemployment insurance over the post-war period? Since 1951 - the starting point of a coherent set of data - there has been a steadily falling insurance coverage for those unemployed. While the full details are given in Table 12, the collapse of insurance coverage is perhaps best seen by taking two points: the first year in the sequence, 1951, and the last, 1994.

In 1951, 78 per cent of what would now be considered a very small total number of unemployed (303,000) gained insurance coverage, of whom 11 per cent also drew means-tested national assistance, as income support was then called. A further 11 per cent drew only means-tested help, while 12 per cent gained no benefit at all. Some of this latter group would subsequently be eligible for benefit once their claim had been fully processed.

By 1994, the position had been totally reversed. Of the 2,551,000 unemployed only 21 per cent had insurance cover, and of these 4 per cent also drew income support. A staggering 68 per cent drew only means-tested income support. In 1951, 67 per cent were drawing an insurance benefit only.

The total number of benefit claimants of course tells its own story of persistent decline in job opportunities as the full employment years of the early post-war period gave way to long-term mass unemployment. Any benefit system is likely to perform differently during such sharply contrasting periods. Moreover, an insurance system where rules for eligibility to benefit were tightened as unemployment rose is obviously going to push more of the jobless on to means-tested assistance.

- **The lessons**

Tighter rules work against claimants taking risks in an attempt to win back a place at work. The Gregg/Wadsworth findings cited earlier are crucial here. Re-entry jobs offer far less security than other posts. Is it sensible to go to all the bother of taking a job which might disappear after a few months, which probably pays badly, and which does little or nothing to help to requalify for insurance benefit? Generally speaking, a claimant requires two years' contributions to qualify for benefit. Under the present rules the scales are weighted heavily against taking any risk and one aim of the reconstruction must be to weight the scales in the opposite direction.

Table 12: Number and percentage of claimants by benefit entitlement(f)   *thousands*

Year	Total unemployment count(a)	Unemployment benefit only(b)		Unemployment benefit and IS/SB/NA (c)		IS/SB/NA only (d)		No benefit (e)	
1951	303	202	*67%*	33	*11%*	32	*11%*	36	*12%*
1952	400	269	*67%*	59	*15%*	41	*10%*	31	*8%*
1953	322	167	*52%*	48	*15%*	45	*14%*	62	*19%*
1954	256	118	*46%*	30	*12%*	50	*20%*	58	*23%*
1955	216	101	*47%*	20	*9%*	40	*19%*	55	*25%*
1956	297	138	*46%*	30	*10%*	42	*14%*	87	*29%*
1957	335	161	*48%*	41	*12%*	55	*16%*	79	*23%*
1958	532	268	*50%*	66	*12%*	85	*16%*	113	*21%*
1959	421	199	*47%*	42	*10%*	113	*27%*	67	*16%*
1960	365	146	*40%*	31	*8%*	97	*27%*	91	*25%*
1961	389	174	*45%*	29	*7%*	102	*26%*	85	*22%*
1962	566	258	*46%*	55	*10%*	147	*26%*	106	*19%*
1963	460	208	*45%*	46	*10%*	139	*30%*	67	*15%*
1964	349	146	*42%*	26	*7%*	105	*30%*	72	*21%*
1965	319	139	*44%*	24	*8%*	75	*24%*	81	*25%*
1966	295	128	*43%*	25	*8%*	65	*22%*	78	*26%*
1967	543	260	*48%*	76	*14%*	94	*17%*	114	*21%*
1968	559	236	*42%*	70	*13%*	135	*24%*	119	*21%*
1969	532	218	*41%*	63	*12%*	129	*24%*	122	*23%*
1970	576	237	*41%*	65	*11%*	140	*24%*	134	*23%*
1971	736	302	*41%*	94	*13%*	177	*24%*	163	*22%*
1972	873	343	*39%*	114	*13%*	255	*29%*	161	*18%*
1973	621	196	*32%*	58	*9%*	234	*38%*	133	*21%*
1974	546	176	*32%*	59	*11%*	190	*35%*	121	*22%*
1975	808	301	*37%*	95	*12%*	251	*31%*	161	*20%*
1976	1,200	446	*37%*	141	*12%*	413	*34%*	200	*17%*
1977	1,229	408	*33%*	130	*11%*	489	*40%*	202	*16%*
1978	1,283	413	*32%*	113	*9%*	511	*40%*	246	*19%*
1979	1,106	366	*33%*	85	*8%*	466	*42%*	188	*17%*
1980	1,304	489	*38%*	105	*8%*	486	*37%*	225	*17%*
1981	2,195	940	*43%*	225	*10%*	735	*33%*	294	*13%*
1982	2,573	731	*28%*	251	*10%*	1,202	*47%*	390	*15%*
1983	2,864	713	*25%*	253	*9%*	1,539	*54%*	359	*13%*
1984	2,999	750	*25%*	223	*7%*	1,661	*55%*	364	*12%*
1985	..	..	..	..	..	..	..	..	..
1986	3,079	732	*24%*	194	*6%*	1,684	*55%*	469	*15%*
1987	2,752	645	*23%*	152	*6%*	1,514	*55%*	442	*16%*
1988	2,264	504	*22%*	132	*6%*	1,254	*55%*	374	*17%*
1989	1,649	278	*17%*	100	*6%*	997	*60%*	274	*17%*
1990	1,432	251	*18%*	48	*3%*	914	*64%*	220	*15%*
1991	2,048	453	*22%*	102	*5%*	1,212	*59%*	280	*14%*
1992	2,546	545	*21%*	124	*5%*	1,564	*61%*	313	*12%*
1993	2,759	543	*20%*	116	*4%*	1,765	*64%*	335	*12%*
1994	2,551	428	*17%*	113	*4%*	1,729	*68%*	281	*11%*

Notes: (a) Until 1964 average of December registrants, from 1964 at second Thursday in May.
(b) Until 1957, December figures, from 1957 to 1964 November and from 1965 at second Thursday in May.
(c) December figures until 1964, second Thursday in May from 1965.
(d) November figures until 1953, then December until 1964 and second Thursday in May from 1965.
(e) Calculated as a residual until 1964.
(f) 1951 to 1964 not strictly comparable with later years, in particular the split between National Assistance claimants and unemployed receiving no benefits.

Sources: *Annual Abstract of Statistics, various editions*
Social Security Statistics 1972
Ministry of Pensions and National Insurance Annual Reports
National Assistance Board Annual Reports

This point needs to be borne in mind when we turn to discussing the framework of a new unemployment insurance scheme. The other important consideration stems directly from the table, namely the relationship between the drawing of an insurance benefit and the absence of a simultaneous claim for means-tested benefits. The data are clear.

The claiming of unemployment benefit does appear to act as a barrier to the simultaneous claiming of means-tested assistance. Furthermore, it is not so much the level of the insurance benefit as the fact of claiming the benefit which appears to prevent claimants becoming embroiled in means-tested assistance.

Traditionally, it has been held that the only way to secure a fall in the number of means-tested claimants is to pay insurance benefits at a higher level than offered by means-tested support. But the figures in the table suggest otherwise. Few claim means-tests with their insurance benefit. In today's labour market an insurance scheme allows partners to work. It is by this means that the household income is taken above means-tested eligibility levels.

The mechanics whereby means-tested assistance plays a determining role in deciding which households have workers, and which households do not, have already been touched upon in Section III. An unemployed person on insurance benefit is entitled to little or no income support. No claim is made if the partner is working, for that partner's income usually nullifies any benefit entitlement. The overwhelming majority of partners wish to continue working and, given that the unemployed partner is drawing an insurance benefit and therefore contributing to household finances, usually remains in work.

Moreover no claim is made by most of these households for housing benefit. Here a number of motives are at work. Some claimants would have been claiming housing benefit in work because of their low income. Their actions remain unaffected by unemployment, other than that they may gain a higher housing benefit payment.

Some claimants will be ignorant of their possible right to benefit and therefore make no claim. Other unemployed claimants, whose partners are working, make no claim as they believe - usually rightly - that their housing benefit entitlement would be small or non-existent.

- **The case for change**

The kaleidoscope of reactions to claiming means-tested benefit is transformed when the unemployed claimant's entitlement to insurance benefit is exhausted. Here all the pressures are on claiming means-tested income support and housing benefit. These pressures are graphically described in a letter written to me after **The Sun** presented to readers the arguments in **Making Welfare Work**.

I am 59 years of age and was made redundant in August, 1994 (this was the 7th time I have been made redundant since 1976).

In the past I have always managed to obtain employment, mainly due to my knowledge and management skills. However, I have applied, written, and telephoned over 300 companies during the past 10 months seeking any form of employment (even down to collecting empty trolleys at supermarkets or cleaning offices/factories) without success, due mainly to my age ...

My wife and I have always been great believers in helping ourselves as against making claims against the state and, therefore, when I was unemployed in the past we used our savings, plus our then borrowing power, to pay our bills, rather than claim benefits. This obviously has meant that we have not had a holiday for over ten years.

My wife and I would like to continue in doing all possible to help ourselves but as the system stands at the present time we are not entitled to any benefits due to her working, no matter how small her income ...

At present we are having to borrow money to repay our hire purchase on the car (a motor car is essential as there is no public transport either from our village, or in fact from Colchester to my wife's place of work) proper food and mortgage capital. We feel it has been essential to keep up our mortgage payments as we only have another three years outstanding, and after struggling to keep up payments, bearing in mind the number of times I have been made redundant, it would kill us both to have the property repossessed at this stage. We have already had to live through the loss of our two daughters in 1969, and the loss of our home now would be more than we could stand ...

My wife presently works between 40 and 48 hours a week and has a net wage of an average of £100 per week ... We were advised by the Benefit Agency that, due to my wife working over 16 hours per week, once my unemployment benefit ceases in August 1995, we will have to exist on her wage, or, as suggested by the social benefits and employment offices, my wife should cease work and my claim for benefit will be considered ...

Both the employment and social benefit offices suggested that my wife cease work in order that I can claim benefits. I feel that this is a ridiculous state of affairs as economically it is far better to say, as I will be over 60 years of age from September, either continue to pay me unemployment benefit and mortgage interest, ie instead of paying me say £140 a week I would only receive say £50 a week. This is a saving of over £4500 a year.

Over the past few months I have written to Mr Major, Mr Lilley, Mr Portillo (then Employment Secretary) and Mr Aitken (then Chief Secretary to the Treasury) regarding the above and pointing out the stupidity of making my wife cease work in order that I can receive treble in benefits ...

This correspondent from Colchester emphasises two crucial and related considerations for the development of policy. The first is the madness of offering perhaps three times the level of help to this unemployed person, but only if his wife stops working. How much better he argues for him to claim only £50 rather than £150. It saves the taxpayer something like £4500 a year. And, because his wife continues to work, he is looking for a job which pays more than his unemployment benefit, which is far less than the size of wage packet he would be seeking to improve on the household's benefit level. When we come to design a new unemployment insurance we must keep this idea at the centre of our considerations.

The Colchester correspondent puts a human face on the two-wage/no-wage household. The pay of jobs open to those re-entering the job market has fallen in real terms since 1979. The pay offered may be of the kind which someone on unemployment benefit (£48.25) would consider. Two-thirds of job openings offer pay of less than £75 a week. The unemployed claimant from Colchester is offered £150 a week providing his wife stops working. As this is 50 per cent more than she earns the economic pressures on her to fall into line and become unemployed are considerable.

Once she is unemployed, her husband will still be looking for work from a pool of jobs the overwhelming majority of which pay less than £75 a week. But now, instead of seeking a replacement for a £48.25 unemployment benefit, he needs a job which, after deductions of tax and national insurance as well as expenses to work, pays more than the household's £150 a week tax-free benefit from income support and housing benefit. Little wonder then that, once the benefit system has pulled the employed partner out of work, and both the partners exist on means-tested benefits, the haul back into employment proves too difficult and financially so disadvantageous that more and more couples cease to struggle.

Here are both the genesis and the dynamics of the growing two-wage/no-wage household division. **Making Welfare Work** proposed a welfare reconstruction which directly tackled welfare's destructiveness of human effort and dignity.

The system should be one that backs effort and should reward those taking risks when trying to get back to work. The seriousness of the correspondent from Colchester is seen especially in the passages where he describes using up household savings and credit to prevent him and his wife falling on to means-tested help. Again a primary aim of the new scheme must be to see that such behaviour is rewarded and not, as at present, penalised.

- **The new benefit**

What strategy should underpin a reconstruction of unemployment insurance? First, the analysis presented here argues for the primacy of comprehensive coverage over the level of the benefit payments. The rate at which the benefit is paid is not without importance. But if the major aim of the reform is to prevent individuals and families claiming means-tested assistance, the current level of benefit achieves this end. The figures in the table show that the claiming of unemployment benefit keeps most claimants off means-tested assistance, but only as long as unemployment benefit lasts. Hence the need for reform.

The second underpinning belief concerns the length for which the benefit should be paid. The Government is reducing the length of unemployment benefit eligibility from 12 to 6 months and renaming the benefit the Jobseekers Allowance. Their argument is that two-thirds of the unemployed are back in work before the 6 months' threshold is crossed. The Government Actuary has costed a 6-month eligibility for a new benefit. The case for a 6 months' duration of the new benefit is the one favoured here, but the Government Actuary's costs should mark the start not the conclusion of the public debate.

The third and perhaps most significant consideration centres on the re-entry to the insurance system once a benefit entitlement has been exhausted. For a multiplicity of reasons **Making Welfare Work** argued for a speedy re-entry into benefit, moving away from what is in effect now a two-year period in work for the restoration of insurance entitlement towards a more flexible entitlement which operated, for example, under the 1911 Act. Claimants were then eligible for benefit providing that 26 contributions had been made in the previous five years. The reform proposed here therefore tries to take into account how the labour market now operates for those entering or attempting to re-enter it.

What is proposed here is a 13-week period back in work and paying contributions before entitlement for a three-month duration of insurance benefit is restored. Those with fuller insurance records, or those who have been unemployed but who have been back in work for six months, will gain a six-month eligibility for insurance cover.

The whole emphasis will therefore be shifted from playing safe and remaining on benefit towards claimants taking a risk to get back into work. Jobs may be difficult to gain and their duration may be questionable. But once back in a job the worker has a chance to prove his or her worth to that employer, and is that much nearer to finding out about other employment opportunities.

In this way the new benefit system will reflect the dynamics of the growing instability of employment for large numbers of workers by protecting the household income of those employed by the payment of insurance benefit. The rules will be turned a full 180 degrees. Instead of a system which pulls partners down into unemployment, and penalises those who take risks in getting back into the labour market, the rules will encourage partners to remain in work and reward those who make the effort to take the risk to get back into work.

A note of caution needs to be added to this discussion. Working the benefit system has not only become a way of life for armies of claimants, it is also an activity which gains passive support from some sections of the public. Voters understand that under the present welfare state this is the best and possibly only option open to many claimants. **Making Welfare Work's** proposals were also aimed at changing this public perception into a realisation that there now is a constructive alternative to working the system, and thereby harnessing the support the public should give to a reconstruction which offers claimants a new insurance-based deal.

Making Welfare Work's proposals took into account the extent to which today's amoral views on welfare have ingrained themselves in the system. Hence the proposals for restart interviews to commence with the registration of claiming benefit. Hence also the request that all job vacancies should be registered at the local job centre.

With the proposal also to build up a complete network of vacancies - providing a job bank service - this reform should double the number of vacancies so registered. All the institutional pressures of welfare will therefore support the need to seek work as speedily as possible. The change will sanction the actions of those claimants who have always so behaved and make their response once again the norm. The new unemployment benefit insurance will be based on a realistic view of human nature, of how attitudes towards claiming welfare have changed over the past 20 years, and the need to ensure that the actions of those claimants who demonstrate the values of good citizenship are looked upon officially with support and approval.

Unemployment Insurance Reform

A new insurance benefit will be introduced giving insurance cover against unemployment for six months. Re-insurance cover will be gained after 13 weeks back in work.

It is estimated in the DSS Departmental Report covering 1996-97 that some 250,000 people will be entitled to the contributory element of the Jobseekers

Allowance in the first non-transitional year (1997-8). The assumption underlying this level of benefit claims is that there will be 2.1 million unemployed.

It is reasonable to assume that if the new insurance benefit advocated in **Making Welfare Work** is introduced it will have some behavioural changes as the rules will make it easier for claimants to requalify. It is important to stress that in practice such changes in behaviour are highly speculative and are likely to take some time to phase in even if in the long run there is a particular effect. Specifically the reform is likely to have a greater effect on those suffering relatively short durations of unemployment rather than long-term unemployment. Indeed, the reform is aimed to keep unemployment short and prevent people from moving on to long-term dependence. As a result, although the impact in the short term is likely to be limited, it is expected to increase steadily as the newly unemployed are prevented from joining the queue of the long-term unemployed.

As far as the Insurance Corporation's expenditure is concerned the Government Actuary has assumed that the proportion of the unemployed who would receive the new contributory benefit would not increase greatly over the currently projected level for 1997-8 as long as the six-month duration is maintained. If the proportion of the unemployed entitled to the contributory benefit increased to 15 per cent of the total (assumed for the purpose of this exercise to remain 2.1 million) that would imply some 365,000 contributory beneficiaries. This would cost some £950 million in 1996-7 terms, an increase of about £300 million over the estimate on the current rules.

There would be a corresponding fall in the means-tested benefit costs to the unemployed which would be derived from a combination of:

* transferring some people from one benefit to the other;
* more wives continuing to work as more husbands (or vice versa) would be getting the contributory benefit and
* reducing the number of unemployed on the assumption that the package would be an encouragement to work (or less of a disincentive).

The Government Actuary estimates that the increase in the cost of the contributory insurance benefit would be roughly offset by a reduction in means-tested expenditure, although there is likely to be a small net increase as some of those newly becoming entitled would not otherwise have been eligible for the means-tested benefit. One important aim of the proposals is to reduce the extent to which women give up work when their husband is unemployed. If it is assumed, as a consequence of the proposed measures, that 20,000 fewer men would be entitled to benefit payments in respect of an adult dependant, there would be a reduction in expenditure (not simply a transfer) of some £30 million. If we assume that there would be a reduction of 100,000 in the number of unemployed, as no-wage householders gained a fairer proportion of new jobs created, there would be a further reduction of about £365m in benefit costs.

This last cost is the most significant and the most open to challenge. It will inevitably attract criticism, as arguably it is simply an arbitrary reduction in the cost of the package and impossible to justify with any precise justification. Such a criticism of any welfare reform which aims to change opportunities and behaviour is inevitable. In setting the tax rates to cover the reforms in **Making Welfare Work** the Government Actuary has therefore excluded the gains on this front. Here, as elsewhere, in costing the financial package every effort has been made to choose the highest figure for the reform proposals, so that they are not open to the attack that some of the costs have been hidden or that some of the gains are unlikely to be achieved in constructing the net cost of the reform programme.

Organising the corporations

How should these two new corporations, the Pensions Corporation and the National Insurance Corporation, be organised?

The aim of **Making Welfare Work** was not to establish two new corporatist organisations of the type which was such a feature of British politics during the central decades of this century. There is no demand for such bodies - even such a key player as the TUC, once a cornerstone of the old regime, has a general secretary carefully carving out a new role. The emerging ethos is for individuals to have as great a say as they possibly can over their own lives and not to delegate roles to other people, let alone to remote undemocratic bodies, when power can be retained on an individual level. **Making Welfare Work** proposed the establishment of a National Pensions Corporation and a new National Insurance Corporation. How should these be organised so that they fit with the new stakeholder ethos advocated in **Making Welfare Work**?

This stakeholder ethos distinguishes what is being proposed here from both the Singapore Provident Fund and the Australian models, even though both have compulsory pension-saving schemes. In Singapore the government quite openly administers the Provident Fund and savings currently have to be used to buy government bonds. That is how it was set up and is likely to remain. Such a model is, however, unlikely to be supported by voters in this country. They are likely to view a simple transfer of the Singapore model as an attempt by government to keep all the advantages of old welfare - of setting rates of tax and reviewing the levels of benefit - while offloading the tax disadvantage on to voters by way of compulsory savings. **Making Welfare Work** argued that compulsory savings would become a viable option only if the welfare rules were transformed from one of dependence to that of stakeholding.

Similarly, the Australian scheme very much reflects the continuing corporate values of that society. The main advance stemming from compulsion is to be seen in the strong growth of industry-wide schemes promoted quite often and understandably by trade unions. There is, however, no national structure as was proposed in **Making Welfare Work** which would become the organisation through which stakeholders would have their say. Such a body would contribute to policy and the debate on investment strategies which have to be decided by pension funds, either openly or by delegating them to pension fund managers.

The organisational framework for universalising second funded pensions is one, in part, of the Friendly Society/mutual aid model. These will be organisations run by their members. They are quintessential democratic organisations. It is expected that many of the new life-time savings and pensions schemes will be organised on mutual aid lines on an industry-wide basis, or nationally, or for groups of workers by trade unions, or will be based on the firm.

The attraction of this savings model, its ownership, and the level of charges, will be such that savers in other funded pension schemes will seek to transfer to these organisations, unless the private sector radically reduces the existing costs of its products. Many of the new schemes coming into existence to work the universalist policy will be organised from the very outset on democratic lines.

Some company pension schemes have long had employee representation as part of the scheme. Unilever, in giving evidence to the Social Security Select Committee, explained how, on average, every 200 employees elect one pension delegate. At a two-day annual conference delegates elect a 12-person delegation as their part of a 24-person board which runs the pension fund.

The 1995 Pension Act laid down that a third of trustees should be employee representatives. This was a weak political compromise, with the government believing too readily that employers would pack up their pension tents and depart the battlefield if any more radical proposition were adopted.

Now that the role of trustees is becoming more clearly recognised, the move to greater democratisation of pension funds will occur in a way which should hold no fear for good employers. Indeed, as the membership of the National Pensions Corporation will be in part composed of representatives from funded-pension schemes who meet minimum conditions concerning the organisation of their scheme, there will be added incentives to play the role in developing a pension strategy which itself will herald the advent of non-state welfare.

The organisational structure of the National Pensions Corporation needs a full public debate and again this is an issue which will be taken up in discussions later in the year. A starting point for those discussions is that the body is at first elected indirectly by delegates from properly established pension funds. Membership would be based on the value of yearly pension savings. The Government - paying on behalf of taxpayers the contributions of approved groups outside the labour market - would also have delegates in direct proportion to the value of these payments. So too will holders of personal pensions. Arrangements will then need to be made so that members of lifetime savings and pension accounts similarly elect delegates. The consequent general assembly will then be responsible for electing a policy-making executive. The executive will report back to the assembly with its universalisation strategy and with its negotiations with the government on its implementation.

Making Welfare Work proposed establishing a second corporation to begin organising a new national insurance scheme. The body would initially have responsibility for a new unemployment benefit and introduction of a care pension.

The governing body of the corporation will be clearly separate from the existing scheme. It will be a tripartite organisation, composed of employer, employee and Government representatives. Again the distribution of seats on the executive would be determined by the size of the contribution paid by the various parties with the Government's share being determined by the size of the Exchequer contribution. This itself would be determined in part by the size of the payments made for those whose approved status outside the labour market meets with Exchequer subventions. It would also be linked to a taxpayers' contribution on all employee contributions in the 2 to 7 per cent tax rate, as and when this financial reform is introduced.

Making Welfare Work suggested that, in the first instance, representatives of the new board might come from employer and employee organisations, but that the aim was to provide direct elections. The assembly from which the executive would be drawn should contain representatives of those who will benefit from the new care pension. Clearly, most of those benefiting directly will not be able to undertake a representative role. But some will.

We now turn to the last of the three major reforms advocated in **Making Welfare Work,** to transform income support from a passive into a proactive agency.

3. A proactive income support agency

Proactive Income Support Reform One

All claimants below pensionable age will be allowed to use their income-support payments as an educational and training allowance. All these claimants will be expected to draw up career plans and actively seek their attainment.

Proactive Income Support Reform Two

Student grants will be transferred on to a student-loan basis. The loans will be collected through the new National Insurance system. The £1.1bn public expenditure thereby released will be used for expanding nursery and childcare facilities.

Proactive Income Support Reform Three

Efforts will be made to encourage claimants to train for these new care posts with children. The reform will therefore ensure that much of this new budget is spent in local, often poor, economies.

The current income support system embodies the worst aspects of the old Poor Law. Benefit is paid only on condition that claimants remain idle. Income support acts as a great depository for low-income groups. It does nothing but pay out benefit and occasionally check on fraud. It is not very good at either task. The Comptroller and Auditor General, for example, has qualified his audit opinion on each year's accounts since income support was introduced.

Income support is paid through the Benefit Agency and it is this body's terms of reference which need to be radicalised so that it becomes a proactive body with two equal duties. The Benefit Agency's aim must be to promote the welfare of claimants (dropped by the Tories from the legal requirements placed on the income support scheme). Here two functions are involved. Those eligible but not claiming must be helped to do so. Then, for those below retirement age, the Benefits Agency must help each individual to construct exits from means-tested welfare dependency. **Income support must be reshaped into a body which acts as a life-raft taking people back into work.**

Every able-bodied claimant would be expected to draw up a career or job plan, ie set out what they would like to achieve during the rest of their working life. Two groups would particularly benefit from such a change of direction - quite apart from the long-suffering taxpayers who are called upon to underwrite the Government's detachment from concern in this area. These groups are the unemployed and single mothers.

Unemployed

Some tentative moves in the direction of linking claimants more closely with the labour market are being made through the introduction of the Jobseekers Allowance.

In one important respect however the JSA is a move in the wrong direction. It is not so much that the 12 months' National Insurance coverage for the unemployed is being halved to a six months' duration. It is that any adult dependant's additions will be means-tested from day one and the whole allowance for the unemployed person becomes means-tested after six months.

Moreover, while claimants will have to sign a Jobseeker's Agreement, the job search assistance is likely to be available only after some time on benefit. The Government's proposal for the signing of Jobseekers Agreements should be reinforced with offers of work. The best way of achieving this end is for the Government to make it compulsory for employers to register all longer-term appointments or vacancies with Job Centres.

It is these Centres which would act as the hub of activity where officials and claimants will both be seeking a much quicker return to work. The introduction of job banks linking all Job Centres and other public bodies, such as Post Offices, into this national computer network recording all job vacancies, will help maximise claimants' chances of finding work whilst strengthening the hand of officials rooting out benefit fraud.

A Jobseeker's Agreement struck with all claimants should be converted from what the Government clearly envisages it to be - a yet more mechanical test of whether a claimant is actively seeking work - into a personalised programme of building skills, opening up job opportunities and the beginning of career prospects for today's claimants. Such a change cannot be ushered in overnight, not least because the existing skills of the DSS's own staff will themselves need to be radically developed for this new role.

Single mothers

A similar approach should be offered to single mothers. Each claimant should be required to draw up, with the help of their family and friends, together with departmental officials, an outline of their long-term job aspirations. The Department's response to this should be to ensure that relevant education and training courses are available for single mothers to join as soon as they wish. This reform points to how closely the DSS needs to work with the Department for Education and Employment.

The scheme will be voluntary at first. My estimation is that the numbers of single mothers (and others) wishing to acquaint themselves with these opportunities will exceed the ability of the staff in the early days to cater satisfactorily for the demand. But the aim is clear. It is a total break from the present system where mothers with children under 16 are not required to consider work or training. The changes will be to one where single mothers on benefit not merely draw up their own career plans, and are positively encouraged and supported to seek training courses to achieve these objectives, but to take job opportunities as they arise. This reform would, at the latest, affect single mothers when their youngest child begins school.

The benefit rights of mothers undertaking courses would be safeguarded. This will signal another major break with the current system. Present income support rules are that claimants on benefit can undertake up to 21 hours part-time educational courses, provided they remain available for work. As part of the Government's JSA the number of study hours will be reduced to 16.

Under the current system single mothers, and others on benefit, are often aggressively questioned as to why they are undertaking an education course. With the introduction of the new proactive agency questioning on why claimants are undertaking courses will cease. The question 'Why are you taking a course?' will be replaced where appropriate by: 'Why aren't you undertaking educational or training courses as a means of helping you fulfil your career plans?' It is difficult to overestimate the change to welfare of the substitution of this one question for the other.

Under the new scheme no claimant will be prevented from attending a further education course by threat of the loss of benefit. Indeed they will be encouraged to do so. Take-up of this reform is likely to be so large that restrictions will be necessary in the first instance. Two forms of rationing are proposed.

In the first instance, claimants will be allowed to use income support payments only to cover living costs for training courses and further education. The second restriction will be to limit the reform to those who have been in benefit for two or more years and who are aged under 26 years. It is this group of claimants who are awarded a lower level of benefit on the supposed ground that they need additional incentives to seek work. It is only fair, therefore, that this should be the group which gains a priority in opting in to the new scheme.

A balance must be struck, however. While it will be necessary to limit take-up in the early stages of the reform, it is important that there is some inbuilt flexibility as well. Claimants should therefore have the right to appeal to an IS tribunal if they fall outside the scope of the new scheme, but wish to be included.

Those unemployed who have also acquired all the qualifications for the entrance, and who cannot, even with the help of the Department, find a job, will have the right to appeal against the restriction on using income support while undertaking a higher education course. Similarly, in order not to encourage claimants simply to wait for two years on benefit before they can gain access to further education, there will be a right of appeal for those claimants who have been actively seeking work, who cannot find a job, whom the Department similarly cannot place in employment, and for whom a further education course could help both their career plans and their future employability.

But all other claimants under 26 years old who have been out of education for two years or more, and who are not disqualified from benefit (for example, by leaving their last job without good cause), should have the right to convert their benefit payments into educational maintenance allowances.

Here is how one single mother in Kent responded to the idea of turning income support into a proactive agency. This highlights how far the Department's attitude has to change - from one of derision to one of positive encouragement - and a need to respect the wishes of the single mother, or father, to begin courses and work which allow them to continue to give their children a security and stability which they would lose if working full-time away from home was the only concern of the taxpayers - irrespective of the children's age. The letter also illustrates the need to build flexibility into the reform. This mother's next step is a university course.

*After reading extracts from **Making Welfare Work** (**Independent on Sunday**, 14th May 1995) I am prompted to write and voice my support as, from personal experience, I can sympathise with the issues raised.*

I am 28, a divorced parent of four young children, in receipt of income support for the past 3 years. I am vehemently against raising my children with no concept of independence, of working to support oneself, or of realising ambitions. I am determined not to tread the usual path of crime and deceit as these are not values I wish to instil in my children. Within the present benefit system there would seem no other means of progression.

As I am legally entitled to earn £15 per week I have held the position of part-time creche supervisor with the local council for the past 18 months earning £12 per week. This, however, does not reduce our dependency on the state. To work full-time would entail great childcare costs, also spending a good deal of time away from my children. As I am their only stability I believe this would ultimately do more harm than good for a relatively small increase in our income.

Being an extremely talented artist I assumed I had solved the problem. I returned to college to study part-time for a B.A. (Hons) degree in fine art intending to teach and work as a professional artist. A career compatible with being a single parent also provided my children with a stable, educated, employed, proud role model. Ambitions one would assume would be encouraged by the welfare system. On the contrary.

107

I am currently covering childcare, travel and material costs plus tuition fees of £187 per term. As one can imagine this is, in reality, impossible on income support. The staff at the DHSS treated me with derision when I contacted them. No assistance is available from the education authority as the course is part-time. The college is unable to reduce course fees and the access fund is only available to full-time students. I cannot apply for a career development loan for a five year course. Adamantly I have applied to charities and educational trusts only to be informed that any grant I may receive could be deductable from my benefit.

I feel, as a single parent determined to better my family's future, I am by no means an exception. Far from these efforts being supported or encouraged by the present system they are repressed. A welfare system that functions in such a perverse manner cannot possibly benefit our society. As one struggling within this system I passionately agree with the view that payment of income support should be linked to a plan for career development rather than perpetuating a sub-culture of dishonesty and passive dependence on state benefits.

This letter suggests how total the reform in official attitudes must be: from a mind-set which justifies what appears to claimants as little more than petty restrictions, ie local education authority support barred from part-time courses - to an official attitude anxious to strip away restrictions which unnecessarily impede claimants' advance to qualifications and work. Nothing less than a cultural revolution in official attitudes in the entire government machine is required if such a reform is to be successfully piloted through.

Raising literacy skills

The thought of a university course is not something which many single mothers might immediately entertain, but it should remain a legitimate prospect for some, particularly given the increasing facility of education at home which improved information technology offers. For many single parents there is a need to gain the most basic skills in numeracy and literacy. This is particularly true of younger single mothers, many of whom were under-achievers at school, became pregnant before reaching the school leaving age, and so consequently have never been offered a full-time job. For many of this group, and others, there is the need to gain the most basic skills in numeracy and literacy.

It is here that a new proactive income support agency would be concerned with raising the basic skills of mothers of children on income support, as well as of other parents. One or two experiments are already under way to bring parents, often the single mother, into school to help with their child's education. In so doing not only does the child benefit, but the mother herself also begins to acquire those skills which eluded her during 11 years of compulsory state education. The acquisition of these skills then opens up a new range of possibilities for poorer parents on benefit, particularly single mothers.

Making Welfare Work means making work accessible. That means opening new routes back into education, training and employment. Pressure on resources means we have to put what is already available in the community to the fullest use. One of the cheapest, safest and most effective strategies - and one which crosses the divide between social and educational policies - would be to put schools to better use.

This is already beginning to happen. Many schools still offer a wide range of activities before and after school and in school holidays for children of all abilities. The 'added value' of organised after-school programmes is now being recognised and monitored for the first time by Education Extra, a new educational charity, which is also working with schools to develop a new generation of after-school programmes. The aim is, quite simply, to bring after-school activities within the reach of every child as part of a national strategy for raising achievements and enabling families *to learn and earn.*

Extending the use of schools needs to go further than this. As part of the Out of School Child Care Initiative (begun in April 1993), hundreds of new after-school clubs are now operating in primary and in some secondary schools all over the country. But they are slow to grow simply because parents need proof that they are there to stay.

Fully-employed schools

It is in this respect that the use of schools needs to be revolutionised. If single parents and others on income support are to be expected to draw up career plans, to seek training initiatives, and then to take work, it is crucial that they know that their children will be looked after safely. There is no better place, generally speaking, for these objectives to be fulfilled than in school. It is crucial therefore that school opening hours match the needs of working parents and parents on training schemes. That will involve the creation of new jobs which will need to be paid for.

Efforts will also be made so that training schemes are available in the poorest areas which will allow many claimants to train for these new care jobs. This will not only offer job opportunities and so decrease unemployment, but ensure that much of this budget is recycled and spent in the poorest local economies.

The barrier to self-improvement which inadequate child-care facilities builds particularly against single mothers is vividly illustrated in another letter from a correspondent in London. By calling for a 'handup, not a put down' this single mother highlights just how strong the drives to self-improvement are, and just how little the state has to do to harness these attitudes - so that single mothers and others - can direct all their energies to earning a living in a legal manner, rather than disappearing into the 'black economy'.

> *After reading your article in yesterday's **Mirror**, I felt I had to put pen to paper.*

> *I am a one-parent family, due to no fault of my own, I might add, as for the Child Support Agency (a contradiction in terms, if ever I heard one). Well, my 3 year old's father will say he is unemployed so as not to have to pay any maintenance. What I wanted to let you know was my own situation as a one parent family.*

> *As you may be aware, there is almost no pre-school education that's available free to parents wanting to return to work after having a child. I was until last week receiving financial help from my mother so that my daughter could attend nursery which is at a cost of £7.50 per morning, 4 hours in fact, 3 days a week.*

> *I wanted to go to college and study to become a social worker. My*

nearest college for this course was Bromley, but Bromley like many other colleges has no child care facility. I eventually found a college that had child care, Lewisham College. Out of 250 people that applied for their child to get a place at the nursery only 18 succeeded. I was one of the lucky 18 parents. Thank goodness I thought, light at the end of the tunnel. I was also accepted for my Health and Social Care Course. I was over the moon, it is a career I have always wanted to pursue.

I have attended with my daughter at her nursery, as my course does not start until 13th September. She loves the nursery, the staff are fantastic...However they have been threatened with closure over the last 4 months. They have had to raise the nominal fee for the playschool to £21 per week. It was £10. Also the parents now have to take in biscuits and fruit juices. I don't mind this, but I am sure some parents will. Also parents are charged 85p a day lunch, which of course is reasonable but when nursery fees, lunch, fares, books etc come out of £86 per week it is certainly not easy. Fares for me will be about £17 per week. I have to get four buses, two trains there and back, Monday to Friday. Now I am not a person to be put off, in fact I am more determined when faced with obstacles, but if you were a person easily put off you most certainly would have been going through what I had to the last month. I am at the moment trying to get a travel allowance. It seems, as I am not receiving a student grant I am not entitled. What madness. I only want to get off of benefit and back to work. There is no help available to someone like myself. I could quite easily have another one or two children, get more income support for the next 16 years. I want to return to work when my daughter starts full time schooling and I will.

Also, once the nursery runs out of glue, paper, paint, toys, they will have to ask the parents to help buy these necessary items. It is so unfair. The long and short of this letter (mostly long, I know) is some parents are trying, very hard, to get off benefit, and in your own words, we need a hand up, not a put down.

Thank you for taking the time to read this letter.

The proposal for a proactive agency outlined in **Making Welfare Work** is a reform which other countries have already adopted or are busily piloting. Since

Making Welfare Work's publication, the Social Security Select Committee has visited New Zealand where such a proactive benefit agency has been established. Similarly, the Netherlands has piloted this scheme and the government there intends to universalise its approach during 1996. The follow-up volume will estimate the costs of introducing this programme, both in terms of increased demands which will be put on the education service, and the additional short periods of time some individuals might remain on income support while completing a course. Of course this latter group may be offset by those who more speedily leave the welfare rolls.

V: BACK TO THE HIGH POLITICS OF WELFARE

... the centre cannot hold; mere anarchy is loosed upon the world.[1]

The phrase 'the centre cannot hold' is from Yeats' curiously aptly named poem 'From the Second Coming'. **How To Pay For The Future** argues that the welfare state cannot survive in its present form. Nor does it deserve to do so. Yet **Making Welfare Work** and **How To Pay For The Future** detailed how a welfare reconstruction could take place which is faithful to the original objectives of Beveridge. This reconstruction also responds to the new political pressures which will dominate the early years of the new millennium.

'Anarchy is loosed upon the world' by the operation of a means-tested welfare. One in three people living in households already draws at least one of the major means-tested benefits. Welfare's anarchy undermines the value of hard work, effort, savings and honesty. Welfare all too often humiliates and destroys a claimant's dignity. The political response to this growing catastrophe has to come in the form of a programme which offers a new vision that could be achieved in stages.

The dominating role ascribed to welfare moves in cycles. It was Chamberlain, with his unauthorised programme, who, more than anyone, broke the nineteenth-century 'rarefied certainties' of the Peelite era where the belief was that social policy had been taken out of politics. From the level of contempt, expressed most notably by Cecil Rhodes as 'the question raised by Mr Tanner on the important matter of Mr O'Brien's breeches', welfare became central to the political economy. Central because it challenged the conventional wisdom against fiscal redistribution, and central also because some liberals saw welfare as a means of rebuilding an electoral coalition. Welfare has once again reverted from the 'breeches question' where it has laid for most of the post-war period.

Making Welfare Work and **How To Pay For The Future** argued that the welfare debate has now become, to use Jose Harris's phrase, the 'high politics' of our time. It is high politics because an out-of-control budget of £92.5bn is already devouring a third of all revenue raised by taxpayers and is thereby the central domestic issue. It is high politics because the dominant government budget is inculcating and rewarding those very values which strike at the heart

113

of an open, free and prosperous society. Cheating, lying, laziness - these are the rewards for rational economic men and women in Britain's present welfare state. It is high politics because the culture of the country is changing from that which dominated the collectivist post-war period to a new form of social individualism. Stakeholding is about to come of age. It is high politics too because, in an increasingly dominant global market, footloose capital demands adaptable skills. Welfare has to be reconstructed so that much of the £16bn income support budget becomes the world's largest technical training budget. Britain's welfare is the most expensive system yet devised for keeping millions of people poor. From this passive dependency-centred budget a proactive agency must be born.

Welfare is high politics in two further senses. Many of the old forms of social cohesion are weakening or disintegrating. New interests are urgently needed to replace the social gravity of the old order. That new order must catch the direction of change if it is to have any bearing. **Making Welfare Work** saw stakeholding as the lodestar for the millennium. Both **Making Welfare Work** and **How To Pay For The Future** have sought to design a reform programme which offers to renew the old vision of an inclusive political culture in a way which could inspire the majority. Welfare reform must seek to satisfy the interest of the majority in a way which offers room and a welcome for those at the bottom of the income pile.

Welfare reconstruction is high politics too in that it is part of the emerging debate about the future role of the state. As the millennium approaches the state is being downsized. This is partly due to the fact that economic power has increasingly moved beyond the geographical boundaries of the nation state. But the downsizing of the state is also occurring for another reason. With the advent of the industrial revolution, and with the consequent rise in national income which resulted, the majority looked to state provision to help achieve the good life. Now, individuals are increasingly seeing the method of advance as part of and not merely a means to the good life itself. **Making Welfare Work** sought to offer this wholesome impulse a means of fulfilling the wish for greater social autonomy in an inclusive manner. It thereby directly tackled what I have described elsewhere as the growing drawbridge mentality of the 1980s, of advancing oneself while blocking the avenues of advance - or of hauling up the drawbridge - against those behind in the queue for the good life.

All programmes have to be paid for. **How To Pay For The Future** contains the Government Actuary's costings of the three-pronged stakeholder programme. Welfare will cost more not less. **How To Pay For The Future** proposes the stakeholding concept, whereby individuals build up their own lifetime savings and pension accounts which they alone control, a start of a stakeholders' national insurance scheme where benefits are linked to contributions, and a stakeholders' income support system which seeks increasingly to turn lost welfare money into a training and investment budget. The aim of **How To Pay For The Future** is to provide a programme, its costs, its benefits, offering Stakeholders an increasing control of their own and their families' destiny.

VI: FINANCIAL SUMMARY

The proposed changes would:

(i)   split the current National Insurance Fund into two parts by moving the Basic Pension to a separate contributory fund (and calling it the National Pension); and increase the entitlement of lower earnings and their contribution liability;

(ii)   cease new accruals of SERPS;

(iii) introduce a compulsory second-tier funded pension, whilst retaining the option to be a member of an alternative occupational pension of at least equivalent value;

(iv)   amend the entitlement conditions for JSA to increase the contributory element and include this benefit in the new Insurance Corporation's remit;

(v)   introduce a contributory Care Pension within the Insurance Corporation's Fund;

(vi)   increase the extent to which the NHS costs are met by insurance-based contributions.

The financial effects of the above in 2000/1 expressed in 1996-7 terms are summarised below:

The split of the National Insurance Fund into the 'National Pension Fund' and the 'Insurance Corporation' will subdivide the expenditure into some **£30 billion** from the NPF and **£12bn** from the Insurance Corporation. A small increase in the cost of the National Pension over the Basic Pension as a result of lower earners gaining entitlement will be offset by the extra contributions from lower earners. Thus the net cost of this change is negligible.

Ceasing new accruals of SERPS will have no effect on public expenditure in the first year, and the savings will build up slowly in later years.

Introducing the compulsory second-tier pension is estimated to result in an increase in contributions to pension arrangements of some **£1 billion** in the first year from those not already currently in either occupational or personal pensions. If this total is split between the employer and employee in the same proportion as the current contracted-out rebate, then the extra cost of tax relief on the employee's share would be about **£0.1 billion**.

The estimates assume that the changes to the eligibility conditions for Unemployment Insurance would have a small net effect on total JSA costs in respect of the contributory and means-tested parts (although behavioural changes could reduce the numbers unemployed). However, there would in effect be a switch to 'contributory' from 'non-contributory' JSA even without any behavioural changes. The change in the contributory Unemployment Insurance is estimated to increase contributory expenditure by about £300 million, largely offset by a corresponding fall in means-tested benefit costs.

The financial effect of the introduction of the Care Pension would depend upon exactly how the current arrangements were phased out and the insured-based system phased in. If all relevant costs after the start date are assumed to be financed by the Care Pension proposal, then Care Pensions are assumed to result in expenditure of some **£8 billion** from the Insurance Corporation. There would be a corresponding reduction of some **£5 billion** in expenditure currently financed by taxation. The extra cost is a combination of insured expenditure replacing self-financed care as well as an assumed increase in take-up of institutional care.

Summary

Thus in public expenditure terms the increased costs are mainly in respect of the introduction of the Care Pension. The financial effects of the changes to National Pension and Unemployment Insurance are small.

Financing the new benefit arrangements

• **Contribution to National Pension Fund**

A variety of possible contribution structures could finance the National Pension.

Keeping close to the current system, and using rounded contribution rates for simplicity, the contribution rates needed to finance the National Pension and the corresponding administration costs are estimated to be 2 per cent on earnings up to £60 a week and 6 per cent on earnings over that level up to the Upper Earnings Limit by employees, and also on all earnings over £60 by employers, with equivalent contributions from the self-employed. If employees paid contributions at the 6 per cent rate on all earnings, a further £2 billion would be payable. This latter sum has not been taken into account in the calculations which follow.

- **Contribution to Insurance Corporation**

The contribution to the Insurance Corporation has initially to cover the cost of the Care Pension, the allocation to the National Health Service cost and the contributory Unemployment Insurance.

As with the National Pension contribution, the contributions needed to produce a specified level of income could be structured in a large number of ways to satisfy various differing criteria. For the purpose of this book, it has been assumed:

(i)   the 'rump' of National Insurance benefits would be financed by contributions from both employees and employers of 1 per cent on earnings below £60 a week and 2 per cent on earnings over £60 a week, capped at the UEL for employees;

(ii)   for the Insurance Corporation (for Care Pensions and Unemployment Insurance part and the National Health contribution), there would be contribution rates from both employees and employers of 1 per cent on earnings below £60 a week and 1.5 per cent on all earnings over £60 a week;

(iii)   for the Insurance Corporation (the National Health contribution part), contribution would be payable only by employees and would be 7 per cent on earnings over £60 a week.

Table 13 shows the effect of the above contribution rates as compared with the

118

present rates of contribution. In view of the switch of the financing of some public expenditure to the contribution basis, the table also illustrates the effect of some assumed changes in income tax rates which broadly offset the reduction in expenditure currently financed by taxation. As with the possible levels and structure of the insurance contributions, there is of course an infinite number of ways in which the impact on expenditure could be reflected in taxation changes.

Table 13a: Current tax and national insurance contributions (1996/97) (£)
Currently contracted-in

Current structure	Weekly wages					
	£100	£200	£300	£400	£500	£600
Employee NIC	5.12	15.12	25.12	35.12	40.62	40.62
Tax	5.52	27.62	51.62	75.62	99.62	123.62
Total tax + NIC	10.64	42.74	76.74	110.74	140.24	164.24
Proposed structure	*Weekly wages*					
	£100	£200	£300	£400	£500	£600
State pension insurance	3.60	9.60	15.60	21.60	24.90	24.90
Insurance corporation	4.00	12.50	21.00	29.50	38.00	46.50
"Rump" National Insurance	1.40	3.40	5.40	7.40	8.50	8.50
Compulsory pension	0.00	1.60	3.20	4.80	6.40	8.00
Total	9.00	27.10	45.20	63.30	77.80	87.90
Current National Insurance	*5.12*	*15.12*	*25.12*	*35.12*	*40.62*	*40.62*
Example income tax	0.95	12.11	31.11	50.11	69.11	88.11
Current income tax	*5.52*	*27.62*	*51.62*	*75.62*	*99.62*	*123.62*
Total tax + contributions	9.95	39.21	76.31	113.41	146.91	176.01
Current tax + NIC	*10.64*	*42.74*	*76.74*	*110.74*	*140.24*	*164.24*

Source: Government Actuary's Department

119

Table 13b: Current tax and national insurance contributions (1996/97) (£)
Currently contracted-out

Current structure		*Weekly wages*				
	£100	£200	£300	£400	£500	£600
Employee NIC	4.42	12.62	20.82	29.02	33.53	33.53
Tax	5.52	27.62	51.62	75.62	99.62	123.62
Total tax + NIC	9.94	40.24	72.44	104.64	133.15	157.15

Proposed structure		*Weekly wages*				
	£100	£200	£300	£400	£500	£600
State pension insurance	3.60	9.60	15.60	21.60	24.90	24.90
Insurance corporation	4.00	12.50	21.00	29.50	38.00	46.50
"Rump" National Insurance	1.40	3.40	5.40	7.40	8.50	8.50
Compulsory pension	0.00	0.00	0.00	0.00	0.00	0.00
Total	9.00	25.50	42.00	58.50	71.40	79.90
Current National Insurance	*4.42*	*12.62*	*20.82*	*29.02*	*33.53*	*33.53*
Example income tax	0.95	12.11	31.11	50.11	69.11	88.11
Current income tax	*5.52*	*27.62*	*51.62*	*75.62*	*99.62*	*123.62*
Total Tax + contributions	9.95	37.61	73.11	108.61	140.51	168.01
Current tax + NIC	*9.94*	*40.24*	*72.44*	*104.64*	*133.15*	*157.15*

Source: Government Actuary's Department

VII: SUMMARY OF REFORMS

National Health Service Reform
Half the National Health Service budget will be covered by revenue raised from the new insurance tax base. The 7 per cent insurance tax will be accompanied by corresponding cuts in income tax. The introduction of an insurance-based care pension will also allow major tax cuts. The examples of possible tax cuts used to illustrate the impact of these reforms were for a reduction in the lower rate of income tax to 5 per cent with a corresponding cut in the standard rate to 19 per cent and an increase of about £400 in the personal allowance.

Pension Reform One
The first move in gaining adequate pension cover is for every worker to be included in the National Insurance scheme so that they qualify for a National Insurance pension in their own right. Everybody earning over £100 a week will be required to contribute to the new National Insurance Fund run by the Insurance Corporation. Earnings from £10 to £60 a week will attract a 2 per cent levy from employees, employers and the self-employed. Those earning above £60 will contribute 6 per cent on earnings above that level up to an upper limit. Employers will pay 6 per cent on all earnings over £60. This puts in place the first building block for an adequate retirement income, ie set at a high proportion of previous earnings.

Pension Reform Two
Workers earning above £100 weekly and not already contributing to a second pension will be required to do so.

Pension Reform Three
Within this compulsory savings framework individuals will be completely free to choose between private-sector companies, a National Savings Scheme and mutually-aided schemes as the

vehicles through which they make their long-term savings commitments.

Pension Reform Four
SERPS will be wound up for new accruals at the millennium. In the first year, the opted-out rebate of 4.6 per cent will in effect be universalised and paid into each contributor's new pensions savings account. Over time those workers not making adequate savings and earning over £100 will be required progressively to raise their savings ratio towards the 16 per cent of income level.

Pension Reform Five
Bonds will be issued to cover the transition cost over the level in 2000 of meeting the accrued SERPS entitlement. These bonds will become payable as the projected SERPS budget falls when a growing number of workers draw pensions from funded pension schemes.

Pension Reform Six
To establish a National Savings Pension Scheme.

Pension Reform Seven
To establish a Stakeholders' Pension Corporation which will have the task of implementing the universalisation of second pension provision for workers earning over £100 a week. The Stakeholders' Pension Corporation will operate alongside a second body established to run as the new National Insurance Corporation. The Pension Corporation's main functions will be fivefold.

Pension Reform Eight
To establish a new savings vehicle which will simplify the operation for the saver while leading also to a simplified tax and regulatory system.

Pension Reform Nine
The extension of pension savings opens up the possibility of

building new mutually-aided, commercially-run organisations owned and directed by the membership themselves. This reform will help recreate a sense of social cohesion in tune with the members' wishes and expectation.

Pension Reform Ten
To bring into pension entitlement the first tranche of individuals outside the labour market.

Care Pension Reform One
To extend pension coverage to all ICA recipients.

Care Pension Reform Two
To introduce a non-means-tested care pension for those requiring residential or nursing care.

Unemployment Insurance Reform
The aim is to provide six-month insurance cover with new qualifying conditions which reward claimants taking risks in getting back into work. A new insurance benefit will be introduced giving insurance cover against unemployment for six months. Re-insurance cover will be gained after 13 weeks back in work.

Proactive Income Support Reform One
All claimants below pensionable age will be allowed to use their income-support payments as an educational and training allowance. These claimants will be expected to draw up career plans and actively seek their attainment.

Proactive Income Support Reform Two
Student grants will be transferred on to a student- loan basis. The loans will be collected through the new National Insurance

system. The £1.1bn public expenditure thereby released will be used for expanding nursery and childcare facilities.

Proactive Income Support Reform Three
Efforts will be made to encourage claimants to train for these new care posts with children. The reform will therefore ensure that much of this new budget is spent in local, often poor, economies.

REFERENCES:

1. 'Things fall apart; the centre cannot hold; Mere anarchy is loosed upon the world'. W. B. Yeats, 'The Second Coming', **Yeats's Poems**, Papermac, London, 1989.

2. A. L. Bowley, **The Nature and Purpose of the Measurement of Social Phenomena**, P. S. King, London, 1923.

3. Nicholas Bosanquet, **Public Spending into the Millennium**, Social Market Foundation, London, 1995.

4. Paul Gregg and Jonathan Wadsworth, 'A Short History of Labour Turnover, Job Tenure, and Job Security, 1975-93', **Oxford Review of Economic Policy, Vol. 11, No. 1.,** Oxford, Spring 1995, pages 73-90.

5. Helen Wilkinson, **No Turning Back: generations and the genderquake**, DEMOS, London, 1995.

6. Martin Albrow, **Globalization: Myths and Realities,** Roehampton Institute, November 1994.

7. Lord Young of Dartington, **A Haven in a Heartless World: The Future of the Family,** Institute of Community Studies First Annual Lecture to Commemorate 25th Anniversary of ESRC, London, 6 December 1990.

8. Hansard, HC., 20 March 1996, col. 238.

9. Frank Field and Matthew Owen, 'Private Pensions for All: squaring the circle', **Fabian Society Discussion Paper, No. 16,** London, 1993, and 'National Pensions Savings Plan: universalising private pension provision', **Fabian Society Briefing, No. 1.** London, 1994.

10. **Social Justice: Strategies for National Renewal.** The Report of the Commission on Social Justice, chaired by Sir Gordon Borrie, Vintage, London, 1994.

11. **Wealth Creation and Social Cohesion in a Free Society.** The Report by the Commission on Wealth Creation and Social Cohesion, chaired by Lord Dahrendorf, Xenogamy, London, 1995.

12. World Bank, **Averting the Old Age Crisis**, Oxford University Press, 1994.

13. **Pensions 2000 and Beyond,** Report of the Retirement Income Enquiry, 1996, Volumes I and II.

14. Peter Lilley, **Providing for Pensions,** Politiea, London, 1996.

15. The National Savings Pensions Bill, [Bill 131], HMSO, London, 15 May 1996.

16. **Redefining Pensions,** Incorporating Unpublished Papers from the 1994 Seminar **Simplifying Pensions**, Prudential, May 1996.

17. **A New Partnership for Care in Old Age,** Consultation Paper produced by HM Treasury, Depts. of Social Security, Health, Trade and Industry, and the Welsh, Scottish, and Northern Ireland Offices, Cm 3242, HMSO, London, May 1996.